Get a Single Life

Get a Single Life

One Can Be Fun!

Liz Simpson

HELP YOURSELF

0-07-139664-0

Library of Congress Catalog Card Number. On file.

First published in Great Britain in 2001
by Hodder Headline Ltd, 338 Euston Road, London, NW1 3BH.

This edition first published in 2002 by Contemporary Books,
a Division of The McGraw-Hill Companies.

Typeset by Avon Dataset Ltd, Bidford-on-Avon, Warks, England.

Printed and bound in Great Britain by
The Guernsey Press Co. Ltd, Channel Isles.

Contents

Introduction

'As a woman proceeds on a heroine's journey, she confronts tasks, obstacles and dangers . . . Along the way, she will find what matters to her and whether she has the courage to act on what she knows.'
Jean Shinoda Bolen MD, *Goddesses in Everywoman*

Single: Lone, solitary, isolated, separate, one. These are the sorts of messages I discovered when looking for words synonymous with the subject of this book, in addition to the concepts of being unmarried, unwed or unattached, which also suggest 'lack'. The insinuation of such words exacerbates the negative attitude of many of us raised in a society that is geared towards coupledom. Being single is looked upon as a state to be avoided at all costs; single people are seen to be somehow sadder, less successful at maintaining meaningful relationships and are not felt to have as enjoyable a life as those who are paired off. It has even been suggested that corporate family-friendly policies discriminate against people living by themselves. Is it surprising, given this reinforcement, that we are conditioned to 'couple up' as quickly as possible, so that we fit in with the rest of society? What of the single woman? We'll look at the negative connotations of this in a moment.

Yet words like lonely, deserted or companionless aren't ones that spring to mind when I think about how I've felt about being single. Nor do they strike a chord with the many women I interviewed while researching this book. In fact, the resounding answer to the question: 'What do you love most about being single?' was a virtually unanimous: 'Being able to do what I want, when I want, with whom I want.' As one of my interviewees put it:

> Compromise is by no means a bad word, but relationships are about compromise and one of the luxuries about being single is the self-indulgence of my day revolving around myself. It keeps me feeling incredibly young. A weekend will come and I'll think: 'I could lie in bed all day if I want to – no one can tell me otherwise.' I can do this, I can do that. It's kind of like being a teenager with that sense of freedom. I don't have to pacify anyone else or keep another human being happy.

Responses to 'What do you like least about being single?' involved factors which occur just as frequently when you're in a relationship, such as not having someone who shares the practical tasks of running a home or not being hugged or comforted when you need to be. If you can get your head around the fact that being single is just different to, not worse than, having a partner then the sense of freedom it offers far outweighs any of the supposed 'negatives'. Not for us the phraseology used by the rejected ex-wife of UK media mogul Chris Evans, who was quoted in one article as saying, 'I'm resigned now to being single for ever.' Using the word 'resignation' implies that the choice of how she lives her life has been taken away from this woman by the actions of her former partner. This is not true – it's her disempowering perspective on her situation that is causing her so much unhappiness.

More importantly, being single is a wonderful opportunity to develop a relationship with the one person who will never leave you – yourself. Indeed, I wholeheartedly believe that you can never have a fulfilling relationship with anyone else until you have first developed one with *you*, and that a measure of the ability to relate to others comes from the extent to which you are comfortable *with* yourself and *by* yourself. Once you have achieved this, there is nothing to fear and *everything* to gain, because the quality of partner you attract into your life means you immediately benefit from the easy, mutually supportive, life-enhancing love of an equal – not someone who needs to be mothered, tiptoed around or handcuffed to the bed in case he tries to escape!

Let's start by defining what we mean by 'single'. When I started writing this book, I had in mind a life guide for women who had never been married, were divorced or widowed, or otherwise without a current partner. But then I began to look at the bigger picture. To me, being single is all about taking control and responsibility for your own life and having the time and space to nurture yourself physically, emotionally, psychologically and spirit-ually. These were the essential messages I wanted to get across and I realised that they are relevant to all women, even those who are currently with a partner. If this situation applies to you I hope you look upon this as a time of preparation for the transition from partnership to singleness that may take place in your life some time in the future. For the sad fact is, even if you stay married (despite the escalating divorce rates), the chances are your male partner will die before you do. We are all likely to spend some time in our lives outside of a partnership; a time that can be as joyful and satisfying as any other.

The implication, from referring to male partners, is that this book has been written for heterosexuals. In a way this is true, since I have no direct experience of a lesbian perspective, but I would hope that the advice given in this book is useful to all women – whether they are gay or straight. My apologies if the terminology used implies otherwise, but it would be just too unwieldy to constantly write him/her or man/woman.

Changing times

We are all part of an ongoing global revolution and, in particular, a time of massive social change with respect to how we view ourselves and the myriad ways in which we choose to form relationships. A comparison of census statistics over the past fifty years, both in the UK and USA, reveals that the number of officially married couples is dwindling. For example, in 1998 the US Census Bureau's Current Population Survey reported that 56 per cent of American adults were married, in contrast to 67 per cent in 1950. Similarly, in the UK, the Government Actuary Department predicts that, if current trends persist, the percentage of married adults will fall from 55 per cent to 48 per cent by the year 2011. It is estimated that the proportion of men who have never married will rise from 32 per cent (as estimated in 1996) to 41 per cent by the year 2021, and the number of women from 24 per cent to 33 per cent.

Divorces are also increasingly common. Until the 1971 UK census, the figures were not recorded as an official statistic. But by 1996 the number of divorced adults stood at 8.55 per cent and is forecast to rise to 11 per cent by 2021.

However, let's not kid ourselves that just because more people are technically single (i.e. have never chosen to get married, are divorced or widowed) there is a downturn in coupling up. Cohabiting has increasingly become the norm in many Western societies, although UK government projections suggest that 'coupledom' – either being married or living together – will become less common in the first quarter of the twenty-first century. Indeed, it seems like the Noah's Ark principle that our societies have abided by for so long is being challenged. According to one study for the UK's Department of Trade and Industry, it has been estimated that by the year 2010, 40 per cent of the British population will be 'home alone'.

However, the fears associated with being single remain pervasive in our society. This is not surprising, according to Victor S. Johnston, Professor of Biopsychology at New Mexico State

University and author of *Why We Feel: The Science of Human Emotions*. He postulates that feelings, like the fear of being without a partner, are illusions, shaped by millions of years of evolution, and that our emotions are intimately linked to our drive for biological survival. If we are not to remain slaves to biological determinism, then we need to more heartily embrace a paradigm shift with regard to the meanings we ascribe to being single, in an age when financially and biologically women do not need to partner up in order to survive. Indeed, being single is increasingly important to our psychological wellbeing since this state – if embraced enthusiastically – can add as much texture, meaning and purpose to our lives as being in partnership.

As you will read in Chapter Two, the whole notion of why we marry, and what the institution of marriage is believed to represent, has changed irrevocably through the ages. No longer is it an economic necessity for the majority of women to marry, nor do we look at marriage as the only framework in which to bring up children. A spiritual perspective has been creeping into relationships in which many people, including myself, believe that partners are companions for part of our life's journey, and do not necessarily need to be 'on board' for the whole trip. Lessons that our 'significant others' teach us should be assimilated, and we should ideally be able to integrate that learning during our periods of singleness before looking for another partnership. However, if being unattached is thought of as a process to be avoided at all costs you are much more likely to make the same mistakes over and over and over again. It's rather like jumping into the first job you are offered after leaving a position that made you unhappy. If you don't take the time to assess where the problem lay – for example, with your physical working environment, the organisational culture or the people you worked with as much as the job itself – then you're likely to find yourself having to deal with one or more of these challenges in the future.

Living and loving

The kinds of loving relationships we take for granted today would bemuse our great-grandparents. Being fulfilled emotionally, sexually – indeed, having a relationship at all – were not the average definitions of early twentieth-century marriages. For many older women, who have or are celebrating the achievement of over half a century of marriage with their partner, quantity is not congruent with a quality of experience in which women are regarded as equal contributors with their aspirations and talents considered as important as their husband's. This is why, although I'm reluctant to write books that are 'gender specific', this one is aimed at women. Publishers may be queuing, chequebooks in hand, to sign male authors willing to write about their emotions and love lives à la Bridget Jones, but it remains a sad fact that our current society does not view single women in exactly the same way as it does single men. Perhaps this is because, through nature or nurture, the majority of females define themselves through relationships, while men tend to do so through their work. Paid employment is the measure against which the worth of everyone in the Western world appears to be judged.

The young women in the TV programme *Sex in the City* may technically be more liberated than the heroines of Jane Austen's books, but the implied desperation to find a partner demonstrates that the spectre of spinsterhood lives on. The word 'spinster', incidentally, has no direct male equivalent given that 'confirmed bachelor' has a much more positive spin to it. Spinster was a term coined in the seventeenth century to describe women who, without money or male protection, were imprisoned in a spinhouse. This was usually on a charge of lewd or immoral behaviour, i.e. for selling to men the only thing they had to keep themselves from starving: their bodies.

Walk into any popular psychology section of a bookstore and you will find far more books aimed at women seeking their ideal male partner than the other way around. Enlightened titles such as Jennifer Bawden's *Get a Life then Get a Man* are in the minority compared with those entitled *How to Marry the Man of Your Choice*, *Desirable Men – How to Find Them* and *How to Meet the Right Man*. We've been entreated to stick to *The Rules: Time-tested Secrets for Capturing the Heart of Mr Right*, and brainwashed by the covertly negative messages of titles such as *How to Get Married after 35 – A Game Plan For Love* (the subtitle, in case you thought this applied to both sexes over thirty-five, being: *A Guide to Meeting and Marrying the Right Man*) and *If I'm So Wonderful, Why am I Still Single?*. All these messages are in contrast to the only male-focused book I have come across: *A Guy's Guide to Dating: Everything You Need to Know About Love, Sex, Relationships and Other Things Too Terrifying to Contemplate*, which sounds much less *desperate*, don't you agree? Later, in Chapter Two, we'll look further at the ways in which the media perpetuates the belief that it's more socially acceptable to be male and single than the female equivalent.

Solitary refinement

How does 'being single' fit into this innate desire for fulfilment, purpose and meaning in our lives? Learning to be comfortable with solitude enables you to find lasting happiness within the security of your own self-love and self-esteem. This book celebrates the benefits of being single for those of us who are unmarried, divorced or widowed, and presents singleness both as a fulfilling lifestyle option in itself and as a means through which you learn to recognise your ideal partner when you meet him. Being single doesn't mean that you don't date, and that you live a loveless, sexless existence and wouldn't welcome a partner into your life, but that it's much better to live by yourself than unhappily with someone else. And, for all the empowered single women I've spoken with (the ones at ease with their single status), being by themselves is not only infinitely more pleasurable than enduring a dysfunctional relationship but also more fulfilling, as the following quotes from some of the single women I interviewed for this book demonstrate:

> One of the benefits of being single is that you have more time to get to know yourself and what makes you tick. My experience of living with somebody in a long-term relationship is that I felt my personal growth slowed right down. Being on my own helped me realise that first you have to grow yourself as a person, and feel what it's like to be an individual, before you couple up. Then, if you do choose to get into a relationship, you have the maturity to let the other person be what they need to be.

> Being on my own I've learned to know myself better, and to be truthful to and about myself. There are always things about ourselves we don't like, and I found that when I was in a relationship it was too easy to ignore dealing with my 'shadow side' because I was focusing so much attention on the other person. Being single strips away at this pretence. Now I'm free to be me. I know who I am and what makes me tick. And do you know something? I am my favourite chum.

> I'm a totally different person since my divorce. I'm strong inside where it counts. I don't feel lonely. I'm quite happy at home. If it's a cold evening I'll go and have a warm bath, go to bed and watch TV there, snuggled up with newspapers, books and my cat. I'm a contented person now and very much stronger. People who have known me a long time, particularly men, have remarked on how strong I've become. As I've become older it's been like I've been on a journey, and that has been a process to become a strong person not in a nasty or hard way, just complete. I feel quite happy and contented with my life which is more than I could say when I was married.

Where I hope this book will be of greatest value and service is in helping you develop more life-enhancing relationships in the future. In his 1999 Reith Lecture on the subject of 'The new relationships', British sociologist Anthony Giddens likened 'pure relationship', i.e. the ideal of coupledom that we aspire to, to a democracy: it is a relationship of equals based on communication, mutual trust and freedom from 'arbitrary power, coercion or violence'. Self-disclosure, Giddens argued, is a basic condition of intimacy. And how can you ever hope to be truly intimate with a 'significant other' until you have explored who you are and what you want? Only then will you be in a position to communicate your needs authentically, because you can only ever reveal what you know in the first place.

This is the core message of this book. The experience of contented singleness not only enhances your life generally, but also your chances of finding love with your intellectual, emotional and spiritual equal. After such a uniquely self-empowering period of self-discovery, if or when you do choose to be with someone it is exactly that – a choice, not a necessity. Just imagine how liberating that is.

Of course, I haven't always held this view, which is partly what qualifies me to write such a book, being, in shamanistic terms, a 'Wounded Healer'. My early adult life was spent lurching from one relationship to another – most of which were deeply dysfunctional and painful, mirroring my own sense of psychological and spiritual unease. I became a classic relationship junkie when I discovered that boys liked me, and I could ignore the demons that needed attending to within myself by devoting all my time and attention to someone else.

I first married as an extremely immature 21-year-old. It was a classic case of low self-esteem. It wasn't that I loved or even liked this man, just that he was the first one to say he wanted to spend his life with me. And while I shudder at the thought now, having grown and developed beyond all recognition since those days, I married him because I was terrified of being 'over the hill' (at twenty-one – can you believe that?), and thought that no one else would want me. The marriage lasted fifteen unhappy months, by which time I had partially come to my senses and left him.

Alone, frightened, deeply in debt and needing someone to take care of me because I was unwilling to face looking after myself, I almost immediately attracted the man who became my second husband. He was my knight in shining armour, a role he undertook – superbly – for about the first twelve years of our nineteen-year marriage. I will always be grateful for, and deeply respectful of, the way he nurtured and loved this rather pathetic, needy, insecure, early version of myself. But something began to change once my two children were in school and I started to write books, appear on television, and establish a buoyant freelance journalism career for myself. I discovered that I didn't need to be 'saved' any more. To my surprise, I found that I was perfectly capable of handling my life and career all by myself. And because I had married with a needy heart and not by engaging my rational mind, I discovered over the years that the vision and values we had each brought to the union were quite, quite different. This was the classic scenario of two people, having shared so much together, discovering in midlife that they each wanted completely different things. We were cohabitees who shared friendship and mutual respect, but, at the deepest level, we were complete strangers to one another.

There's an irony I've discovered from my experience in the two specialisms of work/career and relationships in which I operate as a writer, life coach and workshop facilitator, which is that we choose our careers with our heads when, if we are ever to find our true passion for our work, we also need to engage our hearts. Furthermore, we choose our partners almost purely through our emotions when, for lifelong success and happiness, we would be advised to think more carefully about what we want in a relationship and the characteristics and traits of the person we desire in our life.

Yet, because I continued to live life in denial I didn't recognise that, once again, I was ignoring deep issues which, like dust swept under the carpet, would simply continue to resurface until they were properly attended to. I threw myself more and more into my work, becoming a workaholic – that is, someone who works in order to avoid confronting problems in other areas of their lives. When life decided to kick this crutch from under me I found myself fighting an overwhelming compulsion to end my marriage, leaving my two children in the safekeeping of my ex-husband. Although at that time I didn't know what I wanted, I did know that I couldn't go on pretending this was how I wanted my life to be.

Single again, I immediately embarked on my first affair . . . then another . . . then another, although none of them (thankfully) were ever live-in relationships nor did they involve financial entanglements. I was deeply vulnerable and ripe for getting hurt, but remained, as one of my close friends termed it, 'a repeat offender' – someone who has failed to recognise the dysfunctional patterns in her life and is still looking outside herself to become 'fixed'.

The fear and pain I had to face at this time was so great that I often wondered if I would ever get through it. While all of my relationships, none of which I regret, have taught me invaluable lessons about myself and my way of relating, it is this final period in which I faced myself and my fears by myself, without seeking the 'quick fix' of a man in my life, which has proved to be the most liberating and empowering of all. It is the lessons from this period, the most joyful and fulfilling time I have yet experienced, that I offer to share with you.

I won't pretend to you that the process of becoming contentedly single is easy, although for many of you who come to it with greater self-esteem and coping skills than I did, it need not be anything like as traumatic. And, as you will find with most things in life, there are downsides which you just have to learn to make the best of and accept, such as not always having someone there to hug you when you feel down. Being single is simply a different pattern in the rich tapestry of life and brings with it its own rewards, costs and challenges. However, I sincerely hope, as you work your way through this book, that you will benefit from my personal experience and the wisdom of the other women whose lives I have drawn on, and spend the time you would usually devote to finding out about a partner to discovering what makes *you* tick.

Worldly wisdom

When I was married my world was populated by couples. Now divorced, I have the honour of having a wide circle of friends and acquaintances who are also superbly single. It is from this pool that I have drawn the case history material that you will find peppered throughout this book, which both underscores many of my own insights about living successfully under your own steam and offers practical advice on how to cope with the challenges associated with singleness. This book does not pretend to be a scientific study of being single but contains a collection of inspiring real-life stories and advice to help you embrace your single status more joyously. The reason for including these case histories is based on the benefits of 'modelling'. This technique was developed in the early 1970s by linguistics professor John Grinder and mathematician and psychotherapist Richard Bandler. Modelling is one of the processes within a personal development approach known as Neuro Linguistic Programming or NLP. Grinder and Bandler, eager to discover why some people were consistently positive, happy and successful, made a long-term study of the language, attitudes and behaviour of people who seemed to live such charmed lives. They discovered that by unpacking both the conscious and subconscious mental models of these mentors others could emulate such success by embracing similar thoughts, language and actions.

The women I have interviewed are very different in many respects: they range from thirty to sixty years old, some are from the UK, others live in the United States of America, and they come from a variety of ethnic backgrounds. Some are divorced, others have never married. Some have children who may or may not live with them, others do not. Their spiritual or religious beliefs range from atheism to Buddhism to Christianity.

A number of these women have been parented so well that they innately know their own value and have a high awareness of their self-worth. Others, including myself, who have had a more dysfunctional upbringing, have had to acquire these skills the hard way – through experience. We've had to develop what US psychologist Martin Seligman calls 'learned optimism', in which we've learned first to recognise, then systematically to dispute, long-held distorted or false beliefs about our abilities to handle life's challenges, resulting in a more pronounced sense of self-ownership. After reading Chapter Three, you might like to look critically at your personal narrative – the stories you consciously or subconsciously tell yourself about yourself – and consider how you might benefit from a rewrite! It's not only pop stars like Cher, Madonna and David Bowie who are able to reinvent themselves. We all can.

All the women quoted in this book have reclaimed their personal power to such an extent that they view their lives as a celebration of completion, and enjoy them regardless of whether they are in a relationship or not. Their wisdom is presented as 'stand alone' quotes, offering real-life examples of the issues being discussed. It's worth pointing out that none of these women, including myself, is a man-hater. The majority of us are extremely open to finding a soulmate – a partner who is our intellectual, emotional and spiritual equal – and subsequent to having been interviewed for this book, a number are now in committed relationships. Indeed, none of us regard it as a paradox that we can be sublimely single – enjoying friendship, freedom, travel, our careers, male attention and dating – while remaining open to meeting The One. The two concepts are not mutually exclusive. The essential difference voiced in this book – and we've all come to this understanding in our own separate ways – is that we don't *need* to be with a man to feel complete or desirable or loved. How you can come to this wonderfully liberating state of affairs is outlined in the following chapters:

Chapter-by-chapter breakdown

Chapter One: Where You Are Versus Where You Want to Be

Since invariably we do not choose to be alone, the majority of you may still be grieving from the loss of a boyfriend, partner or husband – the death of 'us'. Only when you understand, and can move through the various stages of loss, are you in a position to accept your single status and begin to move forward with your life. This chapter outlines, and suggests ways to manage, the attendant shock, denial, sadness or depression, sense of isolation, and spiritual 'bargaining' that accompanies such an event. It also explores the difference between love and relationship addiction and highlights four common, negative reactions to singleness which will be challenged in subsequent chapters.

Chapter Two: The Myth of Everlasting Love

A look at attitudes towards single people from a 'big picture' perspective, with regard to the social conditioning that causes us to seek out a partner before we have become fully acquainted with ourselves. We are living in a time when freedom and choice have never been more readily available to those courageous enough to recognise and embrace them – and the percentage of single individuals is rising as a consequence. Because these changing circumstances have occurred so rapidly, the attitude of many people – as highlighted by media pundits who continue to perpetuate the myth that being a single woman is synonymous with someone resigned to a sad and lonely existence – hasn't caught up with the exciting opportunities on offer. This chapter offers ways in which you can deal more effectively with this endemic social narrow-mindedness.

I also offer my own perspective on the nature and spiritual 'shelf-life' of relationships, showing how not only relating to others but also having periods of being single is beneficial to our personal growth and development.

Chapter Three: Change Your Mind, Transform Your Experiences

Countless wise individuals across the centuries have espoused the knowledge that while you cannot change the world around you, you can change the way you experience that 'reality' through the way you think. As Sue Knight, a master practitioner of Neuro Linguistic Programming (the study of human excellence and how to reproduce this in oneself) has recently been quoted: 'It is our thought life and not our circumstances that determine our success and happiness.'

This chapter, therefore, offers practical ways in which to change the way you think about how your life is, or should be, in order to help you create a more fulfilling life for yourself. In this way you can discover that your happiness and success are not dependent on being loved, respected and nurtured by anyone other than yourself.

Chapter Four: Love Yourself, Expand Your Life

In one study of single people it was reported that 85 per cent complained about feeling lonely, proving that this is the most common and painful experience of this particular life situation. Yet, you can be in partnership and still be lonely if the relationship is both personally disempowering and dysfunctional. We look at practical ways in which you can overcome these natural feelings of being disconnected from life, as well as examining how this separation is an illusion in a universe that comprises a seething mass of vibrating energy.

This chapter discusses how being single can improve your social life if you allow it to. We look at ways in which you might choose to expand your social horizons by viewing yourself as a unique human being with specific needs, rather than necessarily labelling yourself as single.

Chapter Five: Discovering and Developing Your Life Purpose

We examine ways in which successfully single women have developed rich, fulfilling lives in areas other than relationships, and discuss the important part that accomplishments in the world of work and career can have in focusing your mind away from others and on to yourself. In the UK it has been reported that the workforce now comprises men, single women and mothers – the middle category being the one most desirable of all because of their enhanced interpersonal skills, dedication and diligence.

This chapter offers advice and exercises to help you find the work you love and love the work you do while maintaining that all-important life–work balance. While recognising that there is a danger of focusing too much on a career, particularly if you are then sabotaging your chances of fully enjoying the many facets that life has to offer through working too hard, my message here is that meaningful work is a bonus that many women overlook. It can be particularly fulfilling for single women, offering a sense of satisfaction and achievement which helps promote greater self-esteem and self-confidence.

Chapter Six: Taking Charge

One of the most debilitating situations faced by women who are not single by choice (yet!) is that of having to make their own decisions, particularly over finances. Learning to cherish your independence and become the power *on* the throne and not behind it is a skill like any other – it can be learned. This chapter will help you address your long-held and possibly outmoded beliefs about your ability to handle money. Money has often been cited as the principle reason why couples break up, since it is frequently more appealing to share one's bed with another, than one's bank account. We explore the growing tendency for people to choose to keep their financial dealings separate – even in marriage – and discover that by developing the practice of maintaining your financial freedom, you can take good money management into a relationship that will not become embittered by battles over who spends how much on what.

Also looked at are the key lessons to learn in ensuring your long-term financial security as well as exercises on dealing with risk and developing your intuition to help you make good financial decisions.

Chapter Seven: Sex and Intimacy

One of the most common downsides for single women is not having ready access to the physical side of a relationship. Aside from sex, singles frequently miss the hugs and cuddles more readily accessible to those who cohabit with a partner. This chapter addresses the myriad ways in which single women can get their sexual needs met, and focuses on one that is little talked about and undervalued as a means of combining sexual fulfilment and intimacy – masturbation.

The latter part of this chapter addresses another kind of intimate relationship – that which, as a single mother, you have with your child or children – and offers advice on how you can ensure that your being single is a positive and fulfilling experience for all of you. The focus on single parenthood in this book is a minimal one for several reasons. First, I don't have first-hand experience of this, which means I'm less comfortable imparting advice that I haven't authenticated myself. Second, there are so many issues around single parenthood which would merit writing a whole book on the subject. That is why, if you are a single mother, I recommend you seek out one of the many excellent works written for this specific audience by those more expert in the subject than I. Lastly – and arguably most importantly – my mission in writing this book is to help women develop a more intimate relationship with themselves so that, at least part of the time, we stop defining ourselves only in terms of having partners or children. All of the issues discussed in the following pages apply to you, whether there are children in your life or not.

Chapter Eight: The Choice of Loving

Living alone and really getting to know yourself and your needs superbly equips you to freely choose an innately satisfying and fulfilling relationship with your significant other. We take a look at what you can learn about yourself from a period of living and being alone, however brief, and the ways in which you can apply that self-awareness to future decisions about the kind of person whom you may invite to share your life.

How to use this book

I like all my books to be practical, irrespective of the subject matter. This is because while it's one thing to highlight a challenge, it's frustrating for the reader if the author doesn't offer some suggestions as to how that challenge might be overcome. The interactive exercises found in the following chapters draw on my experience and knowledge as a writer, facilitator and life coach specialising in the art of self-understanding and personal empowerment. They are designed to tease out what is really going on in your subconscious, in your heart and in your soul. When your embedded beliefs, attitudes and behaviour are brought into consciousness you will be able to reflect on whether or not they are serving the ever-changing and developing person you are. Only then, if appropriate, are you able to change them. This is the essence of the work I do – helping people shift from where they are to where they want to be.

I urge you not to skip these exercises, and have made them as short, enjoyable and immediately revelatory as possible in order to demonstrate their value to you in discovering the joys of being successfully single. Most of them require little more than quiet introspection. As playwright Eugene Ionesco said, 'It is not the answer that enlightens, but the question.' Hence, throughout this book, you will find a series of questions based on the material covered. Their purpose is to help you unpack and challenge some of your long-held assumptions about what you think you want, as well as your suppositions about what it means to be single. In this way I hope to encourage you to review the potentially flawed mental scaffolding with which you have built your beliefs on what you do, or do not, deserve in life.

Unlike money, love and happiness aren't depleted the more you share them around – they are magnified. But the only way you will have a well deep enough to draw from and irrigate your future relationships is to love and be happy with yourself, by yourself. I urge you not just to embrace the theory behind the messages in this book: don't merely engage intellectually when the only way to fully appreciate a new concept is to live it. The tips and techniques included in each chapter are designed to get you to *feel* and not just think, so, for the greatest benefit, please act on them.

Finally . . .

If you're anything like me and the many women I have spoken and worked with during my years as a motivatory speaker, life coach and self-help writer, you will find it easier to make radical changes to your life when you have a compelling reason to do so. One of these reasons concerns your own lasting happiness and sense of fulfilment. If you embrace the messages in this book and undertake the exercises, you will enter, smoothly and painlessly, a surprisingly enriching new phase of your life.

But there is a bigger goal that I urge you to aim for: by changing yourself through positively embracing your single status, you are helping to change our society into one in which women are truly empowered. As such, I believe you will be making as significant a contribution as the suffragettes who went on hunger strike in order to demonstrate their belief in the right of women to vote. You, too, can make a difference.

The life of the single woman has been held up as the penalty for not ensnaring a man as quickly as possible for long enough. If we are to shift this kind of desperation into a form of liberation that the whole of society can benefit from, then we each need actively to demonstrate that being single is an inspiring choice, not a threat. Individually and collectively single women who are happy to be so, can help create this new vision today – right now. Never believe that your act of courage in living your life for yourself, by yourself, is worthless. The difference between the ordinary and the extraordinary is just that little bit 'extra'. This book will help you to discover how to tap into your inner resources to make a truly fulfilling and satisfying life a reality.

If there's one, core message that I wish to disseminate in this book it is that being single allows you the freedom to do what you want, when you want, with whom you want – or not, as the case may be. Once you have tasted this freedom, and have learned to appreciate the different flavour of life as a single person and not as one half of a couple, you come to realise that relating to a wonderful partner is the cherry on the cake – but it is not to be confused with the cake itself, which actually tastes pretty amazing on its own.

The following is my recipe for making that 'cake' richer, more fruity and packed with goodness. Enjoy!

1

Where You Are Versus Where You Want to Be

'Strange as it may sound, the intentional knowing of your feelings in terms of emotional suffering contains in itself the seeds of healing.'
Dr Jon Kabat-Zinn, *Full Catastrophe Living*

Any journey is made easier, lighter and more enjoyable by dispensing with unnecessary baggage. Similarly, you can only move forward to a fulfilling, self-empowered future when you have let go of the pain and acrimony of past hurts. Before you can become contentedly single you will need to have dealt with, and moved on from, your last relationship – or any others that you have failed to draw a line under. Therefore this initial chapter deals with how to recognise and work through the stages of loss that inevitably come after the ending of a significant relationship. Simply bringing the different aspects of the grieving process into consciousness, and accurately naming the various emotions involved, will help you to come to terms with, and integrate, the changes taking place in your life.

Psychologists now recognise that the grieving process is not confined to those whose partner has died. Handling the emotional aftermath of a break-up is painful and frightening, whether what has parted you is his heart attack or his change of heart as to how much you meant to him. Even when it is you who have initiated the parting, it is only human to mourn the loss of a significant other in your life. Inevitably, there's the fear that this will be the last meaningful relationship you will ever have. Alternatively, you believe that life has cruelly conspired to keep you from fully experiencing the 'great love of your life', which you thought (mistakenly) this person to be. With hindsight, we know this isn't true – indeed, we're usually very grateful that previous partners have made way for much more suitable ones – but the terror of such beliefs grips us, nonetheless. Hence part of the goal of this new phase is not about resigning yourself to being alone, but accepting that the person you were with has fulfilled their purpose in your life and it is now time to move on to the next stage of your life's adventure. This point is explored more fully in the next chapter.

Before we look at the five steps we each need to work through at the end of an important love relationship, I'd like to relate a personal story to illustrate the benefits of what has been, to date, the most agonising, yet ultimately empowering, situation I have ever been in. Since this experience, I now regard life to be an adventurous journey in which each pit stop teaches me more about how to ensure that my time here is both joyful and meaningful. This is how I make sense of the often confusing and harsh lessons that relating to others teaches me, instead of constantly avoiding them, as many women unhappily by themselves for long periods of time are apt to do. Bear in mind that experiencing distress is the quid pro quo of life – the price we pay for our attachment to others and to specific outcomes.

Not long after my second marriage ended, I met, and fell deeply in love with, a man who seemed like my ideal partner. We worked in similar fields and discovered that we were highly creative together, there was an enormous amount of sexual chemistry between us and both our personal and professional dealings were hugely enjoyable. I thought of him as a friend as well as a lover –

my soulmate. As happens to most of us, all the work I had done on discovering what my values were, and trying to ensure that the values of my significant other were in alignment with them, went out of the window the moment we met. For example, he was married and I have long had an abhorrence of infidelity. How much more out of kilter can you get than that? In retrospect, I recognise this as an extremely karmic relationship (I'm a Buddhist!), and one I needed to experience in order to grow to the place in which I operate today. But at the time this relationship was being conducted I had succumbed to temporary spiritual – some might say moral – amnesia.

I felt an immediate connection with this man – I'll call him Stewart – from the moment we met. Indeed, our initial meeting seemed to be imbued with incredible magic, as if the universe had conspired to put us both in exactly the right place, at exactly the right time (which, of course, it does!). It was therefore hard not to think of this relationship as somehow more special and significant than any other attraction I had experienced. Having since had similarly magical and highly unusual initial encounters with my lovers – some of which only lasted a few weeks – I now know that these are not prerequisites for finding 'the One'.

Suffice it to say that Stewart and I had an intense, fulfilling, but also deeply challenging (for me, at least), two years together during which time I continually ignored the gaping chasm between my values, motivations and vision for my life and that of his. I'm a very passionate, emotional woman who operates largely on the basis of what she feels. I therefore had difficulty coming to terms with Stewart's somewhat cold, aloof, cerebral attitude towards relating. But I felt so in love with him that I overlooked this key problem. There was nothing more exciting for me than to prepare for his visits or to turn on my PC in the morning and read his loving emails to me. I had become so obsessed with this man and the need to make this relationship work that I doubt there would have been anything I wouldn't have given up (except my writing) to be with him twenty-four hours a day, seven days a week.

US relationship guru, Chuck Spezzano, has written a book entitled, *If it Hurts, it isn't Love*. This is particularly apt for self-love. Had I loved myself more at that time I would have walked away from the agonies of being with a man who was as addicted to the relationship as I was, but didn't even like me enough to end it with courage and generosity of spirit.

To cut a long story short, I switched on my system one morning to find an email from Stewart which began 'My darling Lizzie', which was his term of endearment for me. I froze like a rabbit in headlights when I read the rest of it. He thanked me for the last two years but said he couldn't see that we had a future together and although he was confused as to what exactly he did want, he knew it wasn't me. At first I couldn't take it in. I printed his message off the system and read and reread it over and over, trying to find some glimmer of hope that I'd missed the first time. But this letter was quite unequivocal. Stewart and I were no longer 'an item'.

I immediately drove over to my closest friend, in such a terribly distressed state that I'm amazed I didn't cause an accident, and spent the rest of the weekend there numb with shock. When I eventually got back some sense of feeling, the physical pain was almost unbearable. It hurt to do anything, especially to think. I replayed in my mind our last meeting, in which I had been talking about our future together (note: I was doing the planning, not him), to see if I could understand not just why Stewart had ended it, but why he had done it so cruelly – by email. What had I done wrong? Could or should I have done anything different? Was I so unlovable that I could be rejected so coldly by someone who had meant the world to me? I was literally driving myself, and everyone around me, mad by trying to make sense of what had happened. I asked my girl-friends what I should do, and spoke to male friends to see if there was some gender perspective that I didn't understand which would help me make sense of Stewart's sudden departure from my life. I pored over horoscopes, drew rune stones and angel cards, in the hope that someone or something could tell me that my future would be rosy – which meant one that included Stewart.

I waited expectantly for another message from him saying he had made a big mistake and wanted to beg my forgiveness. It never came. Stewart didn't ring or contact me for six months, and because I was too proud to ask him to come back (or, as I believe now, because deep in my soul I knew that this man was not the one for me), I allowed the space between us to grow. Not a day went by when I didn't think about him or spend many hours crying privately, or going over and over with my friends what had gone wrong – so much so, I'm surprised they didn't avoid me like the plague. I suffered mild depression, although in keeping with my leanings towards alternative approaches to health, I took regular doses of St John's Wort and other natural anti-depressants, rather than going on prescription drugs. In any case, I scolded myself, no one had died. Having always been hard on myself, I didn't see it as justifiable to go and seek medical help because of a failed relationship.

Gradually, I began to clear Stewart's belongings from my house. We had never lived together, but, like most couples, he had clothes, toiletries and some personal effects at my place. I also had reams and reams of love letters and passionate emails to pore over for some clue as to the reasons for his subsequent behaviour, which I thought I may originally have missed. Every so often I'd get so angry that I would have a ceremonial burning or throwing out of his stuff, until nothing else remained – not even a picture. I felt it important to remove his energy from my home, although I would never recommend doing a wholesale clear-out until you feel absolutely ready. A bit at a time works wonders and gives you something concrete on which to vent your anger, which may last several months. Then again, you might choose to keep your ex-lover's pictures, and some belongings, as a physical reminder of how far you have moved forward in the interim.

On my birthday, I turned on my PC and found a cyber birthday card from Stewart. This was the opportunity I needed; not to try and resurrect our relationship, even from the perspective of friendship, which I now realise we never had, but to understand why he chose to break up with me in such a heartless fashion, without any warning whatsoever. New Year was approaching and I desperately wanted to draw a line under this experience and move on. I now knew I could handle anything he would write and asked that he be totally honest about why he ended our relationship in the way he did. My strength and courage, I recognised, came from having undergone the grieving process which is outlined in the rest of this chapter.

Stewart was both gracious and generous in his reply, and that helped me enormously. He outlined what I had already come to terms with – that what we each wanted from life was very different, and that by trying to make it 'fit' we were only making ourselves unhappy and delaying the inevitable. Each day from then on, it was as if a little miracle was taking place. I found that I no longer thought about him during the day. I stopped wondering what advice he would give me in certain situations and went with my intuition instead. Nowadays I hardly think of Stewart at all, except when I meet someone who wants a relationship with me and who exhibits similar traits, or who needs 'fixing'. I am able to acknowledge that they aren't right for me and walk away. I still love Stewart a little but I'm no longer in love with him. Nor, given the feedback I've received from mutual friends as to how his life has panned out compared with mine, would I want to end up with him as a life partner. I wasn't so much rejected by him as protected by the universe from shackling myself to a man whose life mission is so different from my own. How could I ever have hoped to be happy in a situation like that?

The mistakes I had made were glaringly obvious, in hindsight. My core values include honesty, openness and courage. Whenever I have had anything of a personal nature to say to someone, I have done it to their face, even though the prospect might have been terrifying. I never have, and never would, end a long-term, loving relationship by email or telephone. One of my closest friends has always counselled me to judge a man by what he does, not just what he says. Looking back objectively at our relationship,

I could see that Stewart's actions were very different to his loving words and, importantly, demonstrated that his core values were very different to mine.

But perhaps my biggest offence, against both of us, was to try and impose my vision for our life together on him. My professional and personal plans for us were precisely that – mine. And they required Stewart moving so far out of his comfort zone that it wasn't surprising that it terrified him. There was a play running in London a while back entitled *I Love You, You're Perfect, Now Change*, which sums up my perspective at the time: I had fallen in love with Stewart's potential, not the man he actually was. And that never makes for a mutually acceptable, or equal, relationship.

So, what did I learn from all this pain? Apart from reinforcing what I had always known – that to attract and experience a truly suitable partner you have to use your head as well as your heart – I discovered that I could indeed live through (and learn from facing up to) my greatest fear, that of being abandoned by someone I love. In addition, I learned the following important lessons:

- That getting over a broken love affair is a process that can't be rushed. No matter how eager I was for the pain to go away and to be able to forget about this man, it took almost nine months before I started looking forwards and not backwards.
- That healing can only commence when you begin to forgive, even if you can't yet forget. It was vital for me to find compassion for a human being whose only fault was that he wasn't like me and didn't want what I wanted out of life. Only when you are compassionate towards others can you be truly compassionate towards yourself.
- That it's crucially important to integrate into your life what your experiences have taught you, so that the quality of your future relationships can be so much more fulfilling. In retrospect, I realised that I had chosen to ignore many warning signs, including a deep unhappiness at soul-level. Because I failed to be kinder to myself by voluntarily walking away from this relationship, life forced the change on me. When this

GET A SINGLE LIFE

happened, the result was much more dramatic than if I'd faced up to the fact that this person wasn't The One after all.

- Most of all, I learned that no one else could ever hurt me in the same way again, because, in order to survive such a painful rebuffal by another, I had to both love and look after myself very well indeed. That was when I began to learn to be contentedly single. And for that I owe Stewart a deep gratitude.

As a spiritual being in human form (not a human being trying to be spiritual), I believe that my personal growth is paramount. My particular Buddhist philosophy on life leads me to accept that I'm here on this earth to learn certain lessons, each of which takes me closer to the ultimate, blissful state of enlightenment. I believe people come into our lives to help facilitate the learning of those lessons, and when their spiritual purpose is complete, then it's time for our individual souls to move on. Of course, the ideal situation would be that both partners realise this process and mutually accept the parting of the ways when it occurs, but this rarely occurs. Until that state of perfection is achieved, we must face the inevitable process of grieving that accompanies any relationship loss.

Let's now look in detail at the five separate stages of loss and how you can move through them as quickly as possible. But please bear in mind that it's impossible to be prescriptive as to how long this will take, since each person and their situation is unique. It took me nine months to get over my two-year relationship with Stewart, and sometimes, the longer you were together and the more dependent you were on your former partner for your emotional, economic, social and psychological wellbeing, the lengthier the grieving process will be. But that's not set in stone. Knowing what's happening to you, and why, will help you enormously. The other bit of good news is that an extended period of singleness will allow you to develop all the above aspects of wellbeing for yourself, so that future losses and break-ups will never be as painful, for as long, again.

The five stages of the grieving process

Shock

During this initial, but relatively brief, stage of experiencing loss you may feel a variety of unpleasant sensations such as physical trembling, an inability to co-ordinate your body and brain, intense coldness, or feeling so emotionally numb you just sit there, staring into space. The fact that you may be finding it difficult to take in what has just happened, irrespective of whether you got warning of it or not, leads you into the next stage of 'Denial'. Indeed, it's often impossible to delineate where one stage ends, and the other begins, in the grieving process. It's also worth noting that not only do many of these stages overlap, but there is also no fixed pattern to them. You may move through them consecutively, but then have a period in which you seem to regress back to a stage you thought you had already worked through. This is perfectly normal, and just means you have a little more work to accomplish – like having to retrace your steps on a journey because you missed something you needed to see on your initial visit.

When you are in shock you need to be kind to yourself. More importantly, you need to be in the company of a loving, empathetic friend or family member who will nurture you. Talking is an important therapeutic tool and doesn't necessarily require you to be with someone who is professionally trained, although if you are recently bereaved I would recommend getting in touch with one of the many counselling bodies set up to help widows with their loss. What is important is that the person you are with is a good listener (and tea maker!) and will allow you to express your fears in a safe, respectful environment.

Don't underestimate the importance of talking things through for your physical and mental wellbeing. We are becoming increasingly aware of the link between emotions and health, and researchers have found that informational molecules (known as neuropeptides), linked to the emotions are in constant communication with our immune system. This gives scientific credence to everyday experience in which, when we are happy or in love, we generally tend to be in excellent health, whereas when we experience negative emotions we suffer all sorts of minor or major illnesses. In the 1940s when psychoanalyst Wilhelm Reich, a student of Freud, suggested that the cause of cancer is the inability to express emotions, he was vilified and his books burned in the United States. However, contemporary psychologists have found that cancer patients who do not recognise or choose to suppress emotions like anger take longer to recover from surgery than more expressive individuals. Conversely, those individuals who understand their emotional needs and freely express them have stronger immune systems and significantly smaller tumours. It is not the emotion per se that is unhealthy, but the tendency to ignore or suppress it.

Our ancestors embraced an alternative, spiritual perspective to the mind–body link, which is becoming more accepted in the West. According to ancient Eastern systems of healing, there is said to be a flow of subtle energy that is moderated by physically undetectable 'valves' known as chakras, each resonating at different frequencies and closely associated with specific organs, endocrine glands and emotional dysfunctions. It is believed that when this flow of energy becomes blocked or excessive a whole range of physiological, psychological and emotional conditions is manifested. By focusing the mind through meditation, visualisation, introspection and affirmations, it is thought to be possible to rebalance this metaphysical energy to ensure optimal wellbeing. The concept of chakra healing is based on the belief that our minds and bodies must act as an integrated whole in order to ensure that our lives are transformed for the better.

Taking action

This is a good time to begin a self-discovery journal in which you get into the habit of writing down your thoughts in an unedited, non-judgemental way, perhaps last thing before you go to bed. Such a ritual is not only another way of ensuring that you don't repress emotions which may result in future disease, but also offers a valuable framework or sense of security, the benefit of which has been largely lost in modern times. The psychological comfort to be gained from ritualised practices was realised by our earliest ancestors, which is why they came to be embedded in our religions and national and social institutions. Even if you reject the idea of writing a journal (and I highly recommend it as a tool for moving you through the grieving process), try and find a daily ritual that appeals to you. You might try bathing in a warm bath, fragranced with balancing aromatherapy oils, last thing at night, reading several pages of an uplifting book, or meditating in front of a favourite picture or artefact. But, from a psychological perspective, whatever ritual you choose, you will benefit by recognising that even in the midst of chaos and uncertainty there are ways in which you can control your life and what happens to you. Rituals offer structure to a life that might otherwise seem entirely topsy-turvy.

Be aware, as you begin working your way through your grief, that everything that is happening to you is part of the process of recovering your Self after having subsumed it within the life of your significant other. Look upon it as the spiritual equivalent of giving birth: the very fact that you needed to emerge from your mother's womb was painful for you both, but not to have done so would have ended both of your lives. As with the birthing process, what you are experiencing now is not so much an ending, but a beginning – the start of a new phase in your life. Therefore it is vital that you are nurtured and protected by someone who will help you achieve the balance between mourning the past and not entirely losing sight of the fact that you have a glorious and immensely joyful future that is yet to be experienced. It's times like these that you need close and loving friends you can count on.

Denial

This is arguably the most debilitating and difficult stage of all – the one in which you refuse to acknowledge that what has happened is meant to be, will continue to be, and that your lover will not return to you. Or, alternatively, you start telling everyone (including yourself) that this person never really meant that much to you in the first place. There is a danger you could be stuck at the denial stage for considerably longer than is healthy if you don't recognise these beliefs to be ill-founded. Even if your partner were to come back, would that make the problems that led up to your break-up disappear? How will clinging on to someone who may not want to be with you, or who serves no further spiritual purpose in your life, help you step more quickly into your future life? Alternatively, if this person was really so insignificant, why did you spend so much time and energy in developing a relationship with them?

When your partner has died, you have to come to terms with the fact that you are denied their physical presence. It is also less likely that their death will knock your self-esteem in the same way as when you have just been on the receiving end of a break-up. For those of you facing the fear of living without a partner whom you may still see or hear about from time to time, there is a tendency to plot or muse upon the chances of getting back together with them. You may begin to talk as if this is just a matter of time. The harsh truth is, it probably isn't. And even if it were, focusing only on that outcome will hold you back from the emotional, psychological and spiritual development that you need to undergo in order to more meaningfully partner someone, including yourself, in the future.

Denial is rather like saying, 'I'm all right' to your fellow hikers when your body aches, you've got blisters on your feet and all you want is a warm, comfortable bed. It is untruthful, and unhelpful to yourself and your needs. If you give people a false impression about how you feel about this break-up – that it isn't really affecting you all that much, or that you feel confident that, given a few days to think about it, your partner will be back – you may end up missing out on invaluable emotional support and practical help.

It's all a question of balance: it is neither helpful to your ongoing wellbeing to withdraw from life completely for weeks or months on end, nor to force yourself to be cheerful and positive when you don't really feel like it. There is a psychological/personal development technique, which I call 'acting as if', in which you pretend to be imbued with all the qualities needed for the person you want to become. This can help people through specific issues or low self-esteem. From a spiritual perspective, however, this is highly inauthentic. Although 'acting as if' you are someone you are not may be beneficial in the short term, in helping you overcome a hurdle such as a tough job interview, or public speaking nerves, for example, it is wiser to recognise and accept your feelings for what they are – in short, to 'sit in it'. As one of the women I interviewed said:

We live in a society that's so used to instant gratification, and are consumers on so many levels, that we have become emotional consumers. This is why we are swallowing up so many self-help books. We want the answer, we want someone to tell us there's a magic formula which will stop us feeling any level of discomfort. There isn't. We each have to learn to stop denying that life is shitty sometimes, and learn to sit with a level of discomfort . . . just sit in it. You know, life is like a roller coaster. One minute you might be feeling lonely, the next unloved . . . you can have a good cry and then laugh at the ridiculousness of it all because suddenly the phone rings, or somebody does something nice that shows they appreciate you. But we look for a quick fix, and act as if the negative stuff happens all the time, whereas in reality life experiences are cyclical – sometimes good, sometimes not so great. Sometimes rolling with our needy, vulnerable nature and recognising that's part of what makes us a whole person is the most realistic, valuable thing we can do. Once I got used to feeling the whole range of emotions rather than taking avoidance tactics, I soon discovered that even the bad stuff passes and is replaced by something good.

Remember the saying: 'It takes both sunshine and rain to make a rainbow.'

Recognising that you are in denial is an important first step to transcending this debilitating stage of the grieving process. Again, this is where writing in your journal is invaluable, helping you recognise the *real* situation, and not pretending it is how you would, ideally, like it to be. If you are truly committed to laying the foundations for your lasting happiness, now is the time to take stock of what that relationship was really all about. Hopefully, you will have a loving friend who will help by not pandering to your fantasies of getting back together, but who will talk you out of a denial that may be linked to your addiction to relating to others rather than needing this particular relationship and individual. Relationship addiction (and I speak as someone in recovery) is an abuse as chronic as drug-taking, drinking to excess, or any other lifestyle habit that impedes our emotional, psychological and spiritual growth. When you are in denial it's because you fear facing the alternative. You are locked into the past, something that no longer exists, rather than living in the present and hence preparing for your future. Yes, no one denies that your new life will be different. But it's entirely up to you whether or not it's better or worse.

Face the truth – you deserve so much better. And you have the inner resources with which to create a life that is abundantly pleasurable and imbued with inner peace. As you will read in Chapter Three, it's just a matter of attitude.

Taking action

In your journal or a notebook, write down everything you can about your life with this person – warts and all. How you met, when you first realised that you were in love, how he treated you, what that felt like. Write with the advantage of hindsight, and be as honest as you can about what gave you pleasure and what caused you pain. If your fairy godmother could conjure up the perfect partner for you, how would this man stack up? Not just in terms of his physical appearance and sexual prowess, but his emotional style – how he expresses his feelings, how he demonstrates his regard for your relationship through actions, not just words. His sociability – the extent to which he liked, and was liked, by your family and close friends. How he treated waiting staff in restaurants or got on with his co-workers. Examine his attitude towards money, success, self-development and creativity. Was he always looking to improve himself, or was he too busy trying to improve you? What would you say was his philosophy on life? Does he have any spiritual or religious views and how do they match yours? What about morals? Did you see eye to eye on major topics like honesty, lawfulness, fidelity, ethics in business, drug taking and other addictions? Finally, what hobbies and other interests did he have and how far did he attract his own friends into his life rather than tack his social life on to yours?

Now look at how any of these chasms between you contributed to the ending of your relationship. Was the break-up totally unexpected or, in retrospect, can you now see that a pattern of withholding and separation had emerged much earlier? Finally, without wishing to deny that there was ever anything good between you, make a list of all the downsides to this experience – all the things that won't stand a chance of getting past your self-esteem guard in the future. Like his workaholism, incessant flirting, inability to handle money properly, unreliability, bullying or chauvinistic ways.

This is an invaluable exercise that will help you define what is really important to you in relationships in future, whether they be with a significant other, friends, or colleagues and bosses. For that acquired wisdom you can be truly grateful to your ex-partner.

Sadness and depression

Reality is beginning to dawn – and you don't like it. You can't stop thinking about what has happened, indeed you've become obsessed with what you might have done to stop events turning out the way they did. You begin to blame yourself for your partner leaving you – depression being unexpressed anger turned inwards, towards the self. This period may be accompanied by a physical withdrawal from your friends and family, rejecting any help they may be offering because you feel so wretched about yourself and don't believe you deserve anyone to be nice to you ever again. There is a dark, enticing pit which looks so comfortable that all you want to do is lie in it and have someone shovel the earth on top of you. You may find yourself desiring to sleep more because you feel hugely drained of energy, or to bathe several times a day, or you may be so out of touch with your physical appearance that you don't wash at all, and leave your hair uncombed and untidy. Even more worrying, you may find you have lost your appetite or crave foods that contribute very little to your nutritional needs.

As with all frightening emotions, naming them and taking a third-person perspective can help make them more manageable. Becoming more emotionally intelligent enhances your ability to recognise the sensations that occur in your body. This is the time to learn to interpret what your body is telling you. Do a 'body scan' each morning when you wake up to identify where there may be pain or tension in your body. Look for mental and physical relaxation techniques that will help you alleviate it. But remember that these physical expressions of your inner conflict are prompting you to change something fundamental in your life – generally the way you may be suppressing your emotions, rather than acknowledging them, exploring them and then letting them go.

There are days when, no matter how well my life seems to be going, there's a hormonal blip somewhere in my system and I feel down. 'Oh, Liz feels low today, does she?' I say to myself, making an effort to be as kind and generous to myself as I would to a friend who was in the same state. It's then that my inner wisdom – and we all have this knowing of exactly what we need to maintain physical, mental and emotional equilibrium – kicks in, and I stop to make that cup of tea, phone a friend, or go for a walk in the countryside.

It's not my purpose here to name or suggest the various medical or complementary approaches available to help you through bouts of depression, but rather to help you identify how you can derive some meaning from this state and confront, through writing in your journal or talking to a friend or counsellor, the underlying fears and sense of powerlessness that are fuelling it. Even more important, I want to show you that sadness or depression is a natural, healthy reaction to an event we neither welcome nor understand. In the same way that a headache or other pain in the body is telling us that something needs attending to physically, depression is, I believe, a message from your subconscious that something fundamental in your life needs to be addressed and changed. Take prescribed medication to help the symptoms of depression, by all means, but don't ignore the need to also explore its cause.

According to Swiss psychiatrist Carl Jung, depression signifies a 'sticking point' in our lives when we need to get back in touch with our spiritual self and heal ourselves. Depression occurs when you are facing a crisis in your life. According to the ancient wisdom of China, the word crisis *wei-chi* has two meanings – danger and opportunity. Always remember that this part of the grieving process offers a wonderful opportunity to effect positive and lasting change in your life by looking at what you can do to capture a renewed sense of meaning and purpose.

'Take one day at a time' might sound like an old cliché, but it is wise advice for helping you deal with depression. The benefits of fully living in the moment, with its myriad emotions and experiences, are perfectly expressed in the following Sanskrit poem:

> For yesterday is but a memory
> And tomorrow is only a vision
> But today well lived
> Makes every yesterday a memory of happiness
> And every tomorrow a vision of hope
> Look well, therefore, to this day.

Taking action
Focus on the following self-discovery questions and write the answers in your journal:

- Who are you? What are the different ways in which you define yourself socially, and to what extent are these truly reflective of your inner self?
- How would you rate your self-esteem? How much do you rely on other people's opinions of you for your sense of self-worth, and what can you do to change this?
- What is the 'message' to be gleaned from this state of sadness/depression? Look beyond your current unhappy circumstances to uncover the lessons about self-love, respect, assumptions and fears that need to be addressed.
- What can you do today, that is in your control and not dependent on anyone else's agreement or actions, that would make you feel more joyous?
- What are your relationships like with important influences in your life – your parents (particularly mother), siblings, friends? Is there someone with whom building bridges at this time might be helpful to you?
- What unexpressed anger are you directing at yourself that would be more appropriately directed elsewhere? If it feels right, write a letter to your ex-lover expressing exactly how you feel. Don't hold anything back. Then put it aside for a week and read it again before deciding whether to rewrite and send it, tear it up or destroy it in some other, ceremonial way.

Anger

The bastard! How could he have done this to you? After all you had been through together!

Good. Get this out of your system. Anger is one of most socially feared emotions, not just because of the unpleasant physical symptoms which accompany it, but because it is considered such an unedifying spectacle to witness. Having been frequently chastised as children for showing any form of anger, we have become conditioned to believe that people won't like us if we express it, particularly in public. However, although seeing people show anger makes others feel uncomfortable, when expressed in an appropriate way, it helps you clear your system of the emotional sludge we call 'unfinished business'.

Anger can be a positive force, motivating us to take essential action in our lives. It has been the catalyst throughout history for social reform. Doctors now recognise that unexpressed anger can be the cause of cardiovascular disease since people whose lives feature a lot of repressed anger and hostility have been found to be more likely to succumb to heart attacks. You owe it to your health to vent your anger safely and effectively as much as possible.

Feeling angry may be particularly acute when your partner has left you without any word of explanation. Having no ability to communicate your thoughts and feelings to this person fuels the feelings of rejection and abandonment that you may be suffering from. Sometimes, as discussed with the previous stage, these emotions cause us to turn our anger inwards, resulting in depression. At other times, our sense of outrage at having been treated so shabbily by someone who purported to love us is so strong that it's as if a volcano is about to explode inside us. It's at times like these that you may be compelled to destroy all memorabilia of this partnership. In order not to exacerbate your sadness by regretting having done so all at once, it is wise to clear this person's things out of your life gradually, as I did with Stewart's — if that feels appropriate to you.

It's fine that you can't see the good in this person any more. Hold those thoughts by writing them down in your journal. You might like to add to, or review, your earlier list of all the ways in which you were not as compatible as you thought. This can act as a healthy template for the sort of partnership you may want in your life at some future stage. It's only by knowing what we *don't* want that we begin to develop a more accurate picture of what we do want. You can always go over your writings and re-appraise them when you are calmer. But your anger can help you see the true nature of your former relationship without the rose-coloured spectacles that kept it on a life-support system for so long.

A spiritually beneficial way in which to learn more about

yourself, this, after all, being the purpose of grieving your lost love, is to honestly look at what your partner failed to give you, and consider the extent to which you have failed to give these things to yourself. In the film *When Harry Met Sally*, Meg Ryan's character reflects on a relationship that has just ended with the words, 'I don't miss him, I miss the idea of him.' It is within those 'ideas of him' that you can find the most invaluable clues as to what you need to give to yourself. This is one of the major benefits of being single – becoming a fully integrated, whole human being who may choose to share her life with someone, but who doesn't need that someone to make her feel complete. If, at this time, you consider your partner was emotionally cruel to you – and this perspective is borne out later, when you have come to the point of acceptance – then consider the ways in which you are unnecessarily hard on, or abuse, yourself. If your partner was ungenerous, look at ways in which you are mean to yourself, not just financially but in other ways, too. Perhaps you don't give yourself enough time to enjoy the things that matter to you, like a special hobby or pastime. Or maybe you deprive yourself of little treats when you know that it wouldn't cost you much to indulge yourself once in a while.

Taking action

While you are angry with this other person, focus on all the good points about *you* which they have failed to recognise. Take a sheet of paper and start to list those traits, characteristics, physical features and abilities that you are proud of. Don't be surprised if this is harder than it sounds. When one of my brothers left his wife and three children recently, I urged my sister-in-law to help herself work through the confusion and pain by writing an 'All About Me' list. We eventually ended up with twenty items – and she promised to add to this on a weekly, if not daily, basis – but the vast majority of them originated from me. Even the fact that she is a wonderful mother! Use this opportunity, when you are seeing your ex-partner in a harsher light, to illuminate your own special qualities.

Here are some other invaluable anger management techniques you could try:

- Reinterpret your situation by taking a more balanced perspective. Remember what Charlie Chaplin once said: 'Life is a tragedy when seen close up, but a comedy in long-shot.' Try recalling a past situation in which you were badly hurt and angry, then think about how you feel about that event and the people involved in it from your current perspective. Focus on the wonderful lessons you are learning about your tendency to attract less suitable partners into your life and forgive yourself and them for making what was a human mistake – the wrong choice.

- Become aware of the emotions which underpin your anger, such as humiliation, jealousy, fear, resentment and frustration. This allows you to unpack many false beliefs and assumptions that no longer serve you well. What's really at the root of your anger? Deal with that and you'll be able to tackle the cause and not just the effects.

- Engage in whatever relaxation techniques or enjoyable pastimes will help keep you calm. These might include yoga, meditation, guided imagery (visualisation), deep-breathing exercises, swimming, dancing, walking or gardening.

- Alternatively, vent your frustration and anger out in the gym. Try kick boxing, pummelling a punch bag, or body building. There's nothing like increasing your physical strength to boost your confidence and balance your mind. In the film *Double Jeopardy* the heroine is falsely put in gaol after her husband plotted his own murder in order to escape his debtors. She dealt positively with her anger towards him by embarking on a punishing exercise regime which not only made her look and feel better, but stood her in good stead later in the film when she needed to escape from his attempt to bury her alive!

- Make it your daily mantra to complete the following phrase: 'I am angry, but . . .', finding new things about which you experience pleasure and gratitude. For example: 'I am angry, but I am blessed in having so many wonderful friends who love me.' Or 'I am angry, but at least I'm learning how not to bottle up my emotions so that I maintain good mental and physical health.'

- Just give it up. Visualise your anger, and all the other negative emotions that are taking their toll on your physical and mental wellbeing, as an unpleasant colour, aggressive animal, or other unwanted image. Then, in your mind's eye, either dispose of it, erase it, or watch it scamper off into the distance. Try imagining your anger as a dye or some sort of unpleasant substance covering you, and see yourself washing it away under a waterfall or in the sea. You have the rest of your life ahead of you, a life that is potentially fun-filled and glorious. If you want revenge, then achieve it through the most productive means – be joyful!

Acceptance

This is the moment you have been waiting for. It has crept up on you, tiptoeing like a friend, ready to embrace you in their arms. You wake up one day and the pain and fearful thoughts have passed like clouds on a windy day. Your ex-lover is where he needs to be: in your past. The occasional reminder of what you once had may pop into your mind when you hear a particular song, visit a certain restaurant, or when someone thoughtlessly mentions that they've seen him somewhere. But you no longer feel the physical discomfort or mental anguish that surrounded his leaving. You are not resigned to being without him, you have at last accepted that life is made up of different phases and you have passed through a dark tunnel leading from one to another. Now you are truly ready to embrace being single, and to empower your life in ways that – a few weeks or months ago – you did not think possible. You are in a position to give yourself everything that you once looked for in someone else, so that you no longer need a relationship to fill the gaps.

But before we look at what else you can do to break the habit of thinking and acting like one half of a couple, let's focus on some of the fears that keep us believing that relating to others is

WHERE YOU ARE VERSUS WHERE YOU WANT TO BE

our only form of spiritual development. Fears are insidious and can creep up on us unawares. If you are to fully benefit from the lessons learned from the grieving process you have just experienced, or are in the process of working through, then you need to be aware of four common, negative reactions to being single which will be discussed at greater length in subsequent chapters.

Loneliness and boredom

I was inspired some years ago by a friend who, when others were sympathising with her for being on her own at Christmas, replied that she was going to be with the one person she loved more than anyone else in the whole world – herself. Unlike many family situations with their enforced happiness, tendency towards disagreements or full-scale war and general undercurrents of discontent, this woman could simply please herself.

I decided to try this one New Year's Eve when arrangements with some friends fell apart at the last minute and I was left at a loss to know where to go or what to do. Instead of feeling sorry for myself (as I might have done some time ago), I determined to have the best New Year's Eve so far – and I did. I bought myself my favourite food (nothing fancy, just good old homely fare which even now causes my mouth to water when I think of it) and a bottle of the best champagne I could afford. I hired a couple of films on video which I had always meant to see but had never got round to. And a few chocolate treats just in case I felt like a nibble. Midnight came, I wished myself a happy new year and lay tucked up in bed, immensely proud of this unusual rite of passage. Having never liked crowded, smoke-filled pubs or parties, I was delighted to be safe, warm and relaxed in bed. I now knew that if I could be by myself at a time of year when the whole world seems to be relating to others, then I would never feel lonely or bored again. And I never have.

Being single introduces you to the joy of reconnecting with your own best friend – yourself.

Poor social life

I met Sandy, one of the inspiring women whose words of wisdom you will read here and in subsequent chapters, while a friend and I were on a Nile cruise one Christmas. She had booked this holiday by herself, for herself, following her marriage break-up. Here she describes how she decided to take control at what is often a very challenging time for people without partners:

> This was the first time I'd been on a full holiday by myself. I particularly didn't want to be spending Christmas in what had once been the marital home, remembering what it had been like in previous years. I can remember thinking to myself around about October time, 'What are you going to do, Sandy? Are you going to stay in this country and have a really awful Christmas and go downhill, or go on holiday?' And it didn't take an awful lot of convincing myself to do the latter. I booked this particular package holiday because I knew it was important that I went on a tour where there would be lots of people following a full itinerary. So there'd be plenty of contact with others, and lots of social time in the evening to get to talk to people. There was no way I was going to go on holiday on my own and end up sitting in my hotel room or alone on the beach the whole time. Straightaway I knew I'd made the right choice. I gelled with so many people, some of whom were single themselves, and none of us felt out of place or excluded. Everyone mixed so well that it was impossible to tell who was single and who wasn't. So for me there was no problem at all. I never thought I would have so much fun.

Making your own decisions

The trouble with handing over responsibility for your life to another person is that you run the risk of them abusing that power or, at the very least, completely misunderstanding what is right and important to you as a unique individual. The fact is, no one can ever truly know what is best for you other than yourself. You may welcome advice from friends, family or your significant other but this becomes disempowering when you are expected to adhere to it. I have seen too many relationships where women hand over their personal power to men and find that, over time, their self-esteem is chipped away until it is almost non-existent.

Recently I won a trip to Hong Kong and asked a friend who is in a live-in relationship if she'd like to come with me. It was only for five days, but I specifically wanted her company on this mini-holiday because she is fantastic fun to be with and knows the former British colony well, as she used to work there. She was really excited about going, but said that because her boyfriend wouldn't like her going away with another single woman, we'd have to come up with some sort of ruse to get him to agree. It felt rather unseemly to me for a woman of thirty-four to have to lie to her boyfriend about the reasons for this trip, but as I wasn't actually having to do the lying I went along with the plan. Suffice it to say that she didn't make it to Hong Kong with me. Despite her attempt at deception, her boyfriend simply wasn't up for letting her out of his sight for five days and, rather than risking a fight or breaking-up over it, she gave in. Another single female friend stepped in – one who didn't feel she needed to be dictated to by a man – and we had a wonderful time together.

There is a tremendous sense of achievement to be gained from doing things by yourself, as you will have discovered if you've ever watched the delight on a child's face when they first set off on two wheels, finish a difficult jigsaw puzzle, or complete a piece of homework single-handed. By always looking to others, particularly men, to make your decisions you are depriving yourself of a really fulfilling experience – that of taking control of your own life.

Lack of sex life/intimacy/children
The perspective this book takes on these subjects has already been mentioned in the Introduction (see page 17). However, suffice it to say that as someone who has been in a nineteen-year marriage and several long-term relationships, I know it's as common to go without sex and to feel a lack of intimacy when you are with a

man as when you are single. In this day and age when women are clawing back greater control of their bodies and lives and the social climate is changing to support them, there is no need – technically or emotionally – to be in a relationship with a man before deciding to have children, should this be important to you.

Being single is simply another life state in which not all your needs may be met. The important thing to focus on is that when you are in the process of living a balanced life made up of many parts, all of which are fulfilling, then the desire to be touched by a sexual partner when one isn't around becomes a manageable yearning, not an obsession. This whole arena is covered in more depth in Chapter Seven.

Breaking the habit

I conclude this chapter with some inspiring examples of how the single women I interviewed overcame the habit of thinking and acting as one half of a couple.

> Erin: Thirty-seven years old. Writer and businesswoman. Never been married. No children. Has had three live-in relationships with an average four-year gap between each one.

> I censor what I read. My advice would be to gather up your women's magazines and the national newspaper you buy and take a good look at the messages they are giving out. We read articles thinking they're harmless fun, but if you are single and everything you read is about how to have the perfect relationship or how to please the man in your life then that's just going to increase your sense of exclusion because you don't have a partner. Then you will tend to think, even subconsciously, 'poor me'. Some so-called women's magazines are not women-friendly, which is why I no longer buy them. They're written by not particularly enlightened people, many of whom seem to have a huge issue with being single themselves. Don't think that the people writing these 'cosy coupledom' articles have a

clue what they're talking about. If your reading material can't offer positive stories about people who are single, then do what I do and stop buying them. The messages they give out are insidious and seep into your subconscious. If you want to feel positive about being single, read about aspirational role models who are.

Sheila: Fifty-nine years old. Self-employed reflexologist and aromatherapist. Split from her alcoholic husband in the late 1970s and has been single ever since. She has one grown-up son still living at home, who was five when his parents divorced.

I learned to adapt pretty quickly when I gave my first dinner party, something I have always loved to do, after the split. This turned out to be a disaster because I was still thinking and acting like I had a partner and it taught me a huge lesson. When you're a couple it's easy to be in the kitchen cooking while your other half handles the entertaining. When you're single that's not possible. So I had to get my head around – and be more creative in the solutions I came up with – how I could still engage in the activities I enjoy, and handle them by myself. At that time it was quite the thing to have fondue parties or I would prepare one-dish meals like stir-fries that wouldn't take me away from my guests. This turned out to be a lot more fun than slaving away over a three-course meal while everyone else was drinking and chatting in the other room. I just applied this kind of adaptability to other areas of my life and found, once I accepted that things would never be exactly the same again, that tackling day-to-day activities in a new way gave me an immense sense of satisfaction and self-confidence.

Hesta: Forty-seven years old. Management consultant. Twice married and divorced. One son in his late twenties.

I have to say that I found being one half of a couple extra-ordinarily difficult, and part, I think, of what made me so stressed out and depressed when I was married. I had been used to being an independent woman before I married again in my mid-thirties, and had been in politics, on TV, and run my own business single-handedly. I had been a person in my own right and suddenly I was Mrs Somebody and I found that very hard, particularly going to parties and whatever and being an appendage to my husband. And he couldn't understand that. I had to fight to keep my own bank account and all sorts of things, and there was the added pressure of his parents saying 'Why?' because they couldn't understand I needed to retain some semblance of individuality. So, to answer your question, it wasn't that difficult for me to stop myself thinking as one half of a couple. My advice to other women would be to take off the rose-coloured spectacles about their partnership and honestly assess how they feel about this issue. It could be that once you recognise and begin to work through the panic, disappointment, worry, sorrow, fear, shame and other negative emotions that naturally accompany break-ups, you can see the extent to which you've had to sacrifice a large part of your self-esteem in order to fit in with how society expects female partners to behave.

As you will have gathered by now, women who are successfully single either have an innate attitude that they are worthwhile, complete human beings without having to attach themselves to a man, or they have developed this perspective after a series of painful relationship experiences. The importance of embracing this kind of attitude – and how you can do that – is covered later, in Chapter Three. But I'd like to pre-empt that message here by relating how inspirational I've found the outlook of someone who, arguably, is the nineteenth and twentieth centuries' greatest inventor – Thomas Alva Edison. At the end of this creative genius's life, Edison was responsible for well over a thousand patents – equalling roughly one innovation for every three weeks of his adult life – including the gramophone and an electric vote-recording machine. His attitude is particularly relevant here, at a time when you may be regarding yourself as a 'failure' for not being able to hang on to your last relationship.

Because of the high failure rate inherent in all creative activities, Edison experienced a lot of flops – ideas that turned out to be duds. Indeed, it took him over one thousand attempts to come up with the ideal material for the filament for his electric light bulb, and hence convert electricity into light.

What makes Edison so inspirational for me is the attitude he took to such setbacks. Instead of being downhearted, as the rest of us might be, he viewed each failure in a positive way. As he put it: 'I am not disheartened, because every wrong attempt discarded is another step forward, taking me closer to success.'

If you can view the end of your relationship as simply another step on your journey to a immensely happy, fulfilling life then you will put it into a perspective that will help you embrace your time being single much more positively. To help you do that, I'm now going to invite you to re-examine the assumptions that may be causing you to think that everything in the garden of coupledom is wonderful and cosy, and to challenge the myths surrounding the institution of marriage.

2

The Myth of
Everlasting Love

*'With the growth of spiritual consciousness in the world, that model
(of marriage) is being replaced by another: a sacred commitment
between partners to assist each other's spiritual growth ... It is
appropriate for spiritual partners to remain together only as long as
they grow together.'*
Patricia Joudry and Maurie D. Pressman MD, *Twin Souls*

In the days before my youngest brother was born, my mother
used to say that she felt like the Queen of England getting off the
train with her daughter and three sons plus a couple of corgi
dogs. Two and a half decades later, we've certainly demonstrated
other similarities to our contemporaries within the British Royal
Family. Between my older siblings and myself, we've gone through
four divorces and a separation which is almost certainly headed
for the divorce courts. While one of my brothers has a happy and
(thus far) successful second marriage (as is the case with Princess
Anne), another indulges in an affair which has met with parental
resistance and disapproval (like Prince Charles), while I have
fashioned a reasonably friendly arrangement with my ex-spouse,

as have Prince Andrew and Sarah Ferguson.

The lack of lifelong marriages – aside from that of our parents – did not stop my youngest brother getting married recently. Indeed, the next generation of our clan, my children included, are adamant that they will overturn their parents' perceived failures and ensure their marriages last 'till death us do part', as the marriage service states. I can't help but reflect on the irony of such words being promoted by an institution whose early founders, including Saints Ambrose, Augustine, Jerome, Paul and Origen, considered marriage to be sinful, a form of prostitution, a crime against God and a polluted and foul way of life. As St Paul wrote in his first letter to the Corinthians (7:32–33):

> He who is unmarried is concerned about the things of God; how he may please God. But he who is married is concerned about the things of the world; how he may please his wife.

Indeed, it was only in the thirteenth century that the Catholic Church 'invented' the sacrament of marriage. And, as you will discover shortly, marriage ceremonies – which came even later – had more to do with the transfer of land deeds from a woman to her husband than anything to do with love. But I digress.

The message I offer my children, and anyone else who believes it is possible to maintain a spiritually uplifting long-term partnership is this: I sincerely hope that their relationship with their partner remains fulfilling throughout their time together. But I advise them not to count on that being the case. Looking at today's relationships from a spiritual viewpoint – rather than the more traditional, economic perspective – I believe, as the quotation at the head of this chapter articulates, that, in the main, the dramatis personae who populate our lives do so in order to challenge, test and move us on. The most significant of these associations provide the fire with which we transmute our essential being into the most glorious individual that we are capable of becoming, just as a goldsmith's furnace allows ore to be fashioned into a work of art.

However, all too often the human ego overshadows our spiritual wisdom. When this happens we hang on to relationships long past their benefit to either participant, fearing to let go because we are terrified of change and the unknown that accompanies it. This is not healthy love; it is addictive love. It is also indicative of a poverty mentality in which you deny that the universe's sole purpose is to provide an environment in which you can discover unbounded joy. I explain to my children that, if they are committed to making their partnerships work throughout their lives, they need to be extremely discerning about who they get involved with in the first place, and first need to work out who they are and what they want and love themselves unconditionally, before they will be in the right life state to recognise their key relationship when it is presented to them.

What I counsel as much as anything else is that we stop viewing marriage as compulsory – something we do in order to fulfil those needs that we are too scared, lazy or unaware to search for within ourselves. I reiterate what countless spiritual teachers have promulgated across the centuries: that the door to true happiness and fulfilment can only be unlocked from within our souls. It's not an easy message to swallow, given that our society expects us to link up with a significant other, believing that only in relationships do we become a complete and evolutionarily viable unit. The fact is, this is an old paradigm for a past set of circumstances. Life is fast becoming so different in our societies that marriage, in the sense that it was once considered, is as inappropriate today as maintaining the religion you were born under when another – or no belief at all – is more compelling to you.

Changing perspectives

There is a tendency to think that, because we experience and take for granted 'how things are done around here' – what we call our 'culture' – life has always been that way. Take the concept of marriage, for example. For many years now Western women have taken for granted their right to choose a partner who will meet a diverse set of emotional, sexual, social and practical needs – in short, their right to set up home with someone they love and who loves them. Many of today's women also expect to maintain their careers, become mothers and homemakers or to combine the two. We aim to retain some level of financial independence, to choose if and when we have children, or become a parent without committing to – or even knowing – the father of that baby, as many celebrities, like US actress Jodie Foster, have done.

But this freedom of choice, and even the notion that love and marriage go hand-in-hand, are relatively recent concepts. As the *Encyclopaedia Britannica*'s entry on 'marriage' observes, 'Romantic love has not been a primary motive for matrimony in most eras.'

While every culture in the world embraces some form of institutionalised marriage, its original purpose, and what we now expect it to mean as we enter a new millennium, are two very different things. Arguably, the only aspect of marriage (in its loosest sense) we have carried through to the twenty-first century is the notion that without some form of partnership an individual is incomplete, as is evident in everyday references to one's 'other half' – or, worse, 'better half'. Bound up with some religious marriage rituals and ceremonials, is an ideology that states that marriage is a sacred union whereby two individuals are joined together as a single spirit in God. Hence an institution that originally had a very secular set of purposes is given some spiritual significance too – a double whammy, one might say!

However, as alluded to earlier, the Christian Church has taken up a variety of attitudes towards the institution of marriage in the past two thousand years. Because of its original link with the pagan goddess Mari, from whose name the word 'marriage' is derived, the Christian Fathers were vehemently against the formalised union of men and women. It was because of such condemnation that the early churches in Syria decreed that only men who were celibate could become Christian and that any man who had ever married should be denied baptism. In keeping with the fear and loathing of women in Western society that has been perpetuated through the biblical story of Adam and Eve, marriage was thought to endanger a man's soul because it put him in daily sexual contact with his mate. The formalised misogyny espoused by the monotheistic religions of Christianity and Islam strongly contrasts with the celebration of marriage and the act of sexual union in many Eastern philosophies such as Hinduism, which goes hand in hand with the respect and reverence they show for women and our glorious bodies. According to the founders of the Christian Church, the most important justification for marriage was procreation, hence the centuries-long inculcated belief that women have no purpose in society other than to bear a man's offspring.

Nor was the concept of the family, which typically has followed on from the union of marriage, regarded as sacred. Followers seized upon Jesus Christ's words in the Gospels of Luke (14:26) and Mark (3:31–35), which supposedly encouraged people to renounce their earthly families, as evidence that God's Son was against marriage and the family. In contrast to today, when many church leaders and Christian moralists rail against the number of unmarried cohabitees and children born out of wedlock, marriage and parenthood were looked upon as accursed acts. Thankfully for the continuance of the human race, few were swayed by St Augustine's disgust at female sexuality and the birthing process when he pointed out that children are born from a part of the female anatomy 'between faeces and urine'. And this from a man who, before his conversion, lived for eleven years with a woman and fathered a son.

Gradually and reluctantly, the Church embraced the practice of marriage, although its earliest ceremonies consisted of brief blessings conducted outside churches to ensure that God's house didn't become contaminated by the lustfulness of the union being celebrated. So much for the contemporary saying that some marriages are made in heaven. According to the Christian authorities of the time, none of them were. However, the Church recognised that getting more involved in such a widespread activity as marriage offered it a means of controlling civil and political life. As such, it could direct people how to behave, for example insisting on monogamy, fidelity, and ensuring that the female partner – not just the male – gave her consent to the union, as required by the question, 'Do you take this man to be your lawful, wedded husband?'

Later still, and once again in contrast to its position today, the Church actually condoned sex before marriage. In his book, *Marriage After Modernity: Christian Marriage in Modern Times*, British theologian Adrian Thatcher points out that for centuries the Church supported 'betrothal', a period in which a couple publicly committed to marry but which, in the meantime, allowed them to become sexually intimate. That a marriage began only after a recognised ceremony is a relatively recent peculiarity since weddings only became a legal requirement in England and Wales in 1754. Whereas today the number of unmarried mothers seems to be soaring, and many people are shaking their heads and asking what has become of our society, in the eighteenth century the statistics hardly would have raised an eyebrow, since half the brides in Britain and North America were estimated to be pregnant when they got to the altar.

However, this acceptance of the concept of marriage and the Church's enthusiastic adoption of the pagan ceremony with which it was traditionally associated, had little to do with the celebration of the love of a man and a woman, and much to do with male economic domination. In pagan societies, in which the Divine was worshipped as the Great Mother Goddess, women had equal rights to the ownership of land, whereas Christian authorities insisted that, once a woman was married, her property came under the jurisdiction of her husband. From taking over her belongings it was only a small step to promoting the notion that a man owned his wife and, as such, could treat her exactly as he pleased. Indeed, one fifteenth-century friar named Cherubino, who wrote a book entitled *Rules of Marriage*, instructed husbands to readily and soundly beat their women, 'not in rage but out of charity and concern for their souls'. As one nineteenth-century US suffragist, Josephine Henry, wrote: 'The by-paths of ecclesiastical history are fetid with the records of crimes against women.'

As author E. J. Graff states in the book *What is Marriage? The Strange Social History of our Most Intimate Institution*, 'For thousands of years the marriage bargain your parents made for you was more comparable to today's college education than to today's marriages.' It was only in the mid-nineteenth century, when married women started to rebel against the loss of their authority regarding their own property and lives, that society began to give up its insistence that men control everything in exchange for saying they would support their wives and offspring. Ironically, a single woman in the nineteenth century had more financial, legal and civil rights than her married counterpart.

Even in the 1940s, when Christian theologian and author C. S. Lewis wrote his book *Mere Christianity*, the idea prevailed that women were not only second-class citizens but were also only too grateful to be so. Lewis says: 'There must be something unnatural about the rule of wives over husbands, because the wives themselves are half ashamed of it and despise the husbands whom they rule.' Hence his rationale that there should be a head of each household – and that this head should be the man. The long-standing Christian 'anti-family' stance rears its head when Lewis argues that a husband's function is to prevent the natural tendency of a wife and mother to inflict her 'intense family patriotism' on their neighbours. If the family dog bites the child next door or your child hurts someone else's pet, 'which would you sooner have to deal with, the master of that house or the mistress?' Lewis asks, in the tone of someone who considers it unbelievable that it might be the latter.

This kind of brainwashing was endemic. In an issue of *The Lady's Magazine* of the late eighteenth century, it is written: 'The intent of matrimony is not for man and his wife to be always taken up with each other, but jointly to discharge the duties of civil society, to govern their families with prudence and to educate their children with discretion.'

Legal history doesn't come off much better than its ecclesiastical counterpart concerning its defence of the female half of the population. Until the end of the nineteenth century, the ritualistic abuses of women in the domestic environment, which would have carried grave penalties had they been perpetrated against other men, were legally ignored. This immunity from prosecution is as prevalent today. Despite laws that are supposed to protect all citizens against violence no matter where it occurs, it appears that women have to demonstrate physical proof of assault before they can be legally protected in their own homes.

This is the contradictory background on which our notion of the meaning of marriage is founded. Where does love fit into the equation? The fact is, for centuries people have married mainly to perpetuate society by conferring a legitimate status on the offspring of that union by binding a father legally (if not emotionally) to his children, and also to achieve desirable alliances either within or between different groups or tribes. In all of this, the personal desires or wishes of the individuals involved didn't come into it. To love your intended spouse, or even to like them, was not required. Some societies, such as that of the Zulus in Africa, confer such importance on perpetuating the family line (and hence passing on attendant privileges and wealth) that if no male heir is available, the eldest daughter of the family, or another rich, important female, can marry another woman and become the 'father' to children sired by one of her male relatives.

In the French courts during the Middle Ages love and marriage were considered quite separate. True love was courtly love in which a lady – married to someone probably much older to cement some family alliance – would inspire gallantry and deeds of daring in her chosen knight. The passion between the two was often not consummated. However, the Church stamped on even this aspect of society by threatening the poets who dared to proclaim the ecstasies of romantic love. During the twelfth century for example, no poet could receive Holy Communion, and bards and writers of romantic stories were denounced for encouraging men to make ordinary women goddesses in their eyes – a sin tantamount to worshipping Satan.

Because of the system of monetary or land exchange that was an essential constituent of marriage, who you could or could not be joined together with has, for centuries, been socially regulated. Endogamy, whereby one is only allowed to marry within a specific group or tribe, has taken on a new twist in the twenty-first century within the Jewish community in New York: concerned at the number of individuals marrying outside the faith, they have set up a 'closed shop' dating service called SpeedDating. In line with the 'quick fix' society we live in today – particularly prevalent in the Big Apple – participants are given seven minutes to cross-examine potential Jewish partners to find out if they are likely to be compatible, before moving on to the next person.

Before we look at the opportunities to be gained from this psychological and environmental melting pot in which we are living, let's explore another example of how the paradox of change alongside continuity is an inherent part of society. And, in particular, how the nature of culture is socially constructed – and hence can be changed – rather than being a fait accompli.

The concept of 'childhood' and the nature of children as smaller versions of adults with the right to respect and a certain freedom of expression – even economic expression – is also very new in Western societies. The trade of selling children as sweatshop workers in Third World countries is today a cause for international concern and lobbying against the multinational organisations and governments who perpetrate, or do little to prevent, this scandalous situation. In the Middle Ages, and right up to the middle of the nineteenth century when legislation was brought in protecting British children from exploitation, youngsters were regarded as property and, from a young age, worked long hours in the fields or factories.

Similarly, it is hard to reconcile a twenty-first-century mother's love and protection of her children with the fact that for hundreds of years youngsters whose ages hadn't reached double figures were sold to wealthy families as servants and possibly were never seen again. As a parent myself, I'm alarmed to think that my father left school at fourteen and went to work all over Scotland, sometimes hundreds of miles away from where my grandparents lived. I cannot begin to think how my own seventeen-year-old son would cope practically or emotionally in the same circumstances. Yet, were we living in the Middle Ages it would have seemed natural to me for him to leave the family unit to work for some feudal lord, perhaps never to be seen again. Not only childhood but also maternal affection may be a recently invented phenomenon, given that for centuries children died in such numbers that many parents were thought to have withheld their affection from them in order to avoid constant grief.

What all this demonstrates is that we are fighting to establish more personally liberating, flexible and spiritually enhanced lives while still – subconsciously at least – adhering to the paradigms of more rigid, confining and economically focused times. It is not surprising, then, that currently life seems so confusing to many people. It would seem that the nice, neat family unit of mother, father and 2.4 children who live and love 'till death do they part' has more to do with the TV soap operas we've been force-fed, than real life. And therein lies part of the problem: once it was religion and the highly emotive despatches sent down from the pulpits that influenced society, today it is the media. If we allow them to, the insidious, often anti-single (or, more to the point, relationship-obsessed) messages in our newspapers, magazines, radio and television programmes can reinforce the erroneous belief that life is only good if you are coupled up.

Consider this: a brief examination of women's magazines which I conducted both in the UK and the US revealed how much is written about getting, keeping and even proposing to a partner. Relationship-focused features filled a good many of their pages, with titles like:

Who's your dream date? Which guy can make your prom fantasies come true?

What guys will and won't put up with when it comes to
your bad habits
The rejection survival guide
Want more commitment? Take control and make it happen
Men guaranteed: Your 14-day countdown to sex goddess status
How to propose to your man
Make his love last: four sneaky ways to melt a man's heart
Quiz: are your guy standards too high?
Still single? Could the love of your life be right under
your nose?

In comparison, most of the male magazine titles I reviewed centred around sex, interviews with pop and film stars, sex, pictures of partially naked women, sport, fashion, clubbing, sex, drug culture – oh, and sex. Very few of the articles I read in men's magazines focused on relationships, and of those that did, the emphasis was on widening their reader's choice rather than the desperation angles conjured up by their female counterparts.

The messages you subconsciously receive through the things you read, listen to or watch have a powerful influence on the way you think about your single status. But, like the television soap operas, they rarely present life as it really is. What journalists are writing about are soundbite relationships without the warts and – I speak as a journalist myself – many of these articles are written by women who are not particularly enlightened or secure and are offloading their personal prejudices about being single. In the same way that sensible actors refuse to read reviews of their performances in case it influences the way they perform in the future, I would encourage you to take charge and censor what you read and watch. Make sure it reflects how you feel about life and not what a complete stranger is trying to brainwash you into believing.

- Become aware of the external influences you expose yourself to. For example, if you are still feeling vulnerable or sad after the break-up of a relationship, avoid romantic films and novels for a while. Watch a movie about dysfunctional relationships or something like *Thelma and Louise*, and revel in the fact that you are a free woman with a whole host of life choices available to you. Similarly, if you are committed to feeling positive about being single, read about aspirational role models who are, or were, unmarried. Seek out studies that promote your lifestyle, such as the one that found that the health and psychological wellbeing of single women exceeds that of single men and is comparable to, or surpasses that, of married women. Or facts such as this one from professor of behavioural biology Dr Paul Martin's book, *The Healing Mind*: 'The statistics . . . show that on average men derive greater mental and physical benefits from marriage than women.' You can help to change society by modifying your mental focus, which is the central message of the next chapter. Okay, so it's been found that the distinguished women listed in *Who's Who* are four times more likely to be unmarried than their male counterparts. Or that successful married women are three times more likely to be childless than successful married men. This demonstrates that there is a strong correlation between being a single woman and high achievement. This being the case, you might consider that yours is the perfect situation in which to focus on a form of accomplishment other than having a full-time or long-term relationship. Chapter Five outlines the value and satisfaction of creating a working life that you feel passionate about – and ways in which you can make this a reality in your life.

- Enhance your physical environment to reflect your new life. Researchers have discovered that the environment has a profound effect on our moods – it can either lead us into mild depression or heighten our senses. This is why fast food outlets are painted red (a colour with a resonance that causes us to feel rather frenetic if we come into contact with it for too long), and why hospitals and other places of calm are decorated in soft greens and other soothing pastels. Engage in a spot of clutter clearing, in which you eliminate as much as you feel comfortable with of any material that reminds you of a previous phase in your life. Then fill your living (and working) space with whatever sounds, aromas and sights that appeal most to you. Consider the amount of light that you have and whether you would benefit from more natural illumination. What temperature level do you feel most comfortable with? Indulge all your senses in a way that not only demonstrates that you 'own' your space but also generates positive moods and enhances your physical health and wellbeing.

- Think carefully about the relationship you have with couples. Is seeing them a habit left over from a previous partnership you had? To what extent is one of these individuals your friend and the other simply your friend's partner? Why not suggest that you see only the person you really have the relationship with – so that the two of you can have time to explore your shared values and interests on your own? In my experience single women in the presence of couples causes some of them to appear uncomfortable or threatened, hence they indulge in the sort of gooey behaviour that would make anyone cringe. Equally, if it's intelligent, stimulating conversation that you're after, be selective as to who you socialise with. This includes avoiding women who only talk about the men in their life or their children or who moan about being on their own.

- If you find your married or partnered friends have a tendency to try and pair you off with unattached men without your permission, politely ask them to stop doing this. If they don't, you might need to take more drastic action, as Harriet outlines:

> I'm frequently getting invited to dinner parties in which there 'just happens' to be a spare man at the table. Most of the time I just laugh this kind of behaviour off. But if it persists then I believe it's up to me to do something about it. I generally point out that I'm not lonely living by myself, and that if my friends think my life is empty then perhaps that says more about their own prejudices and fears? One friend of mine was constantly setting me up with single men that she and her husband thought might be suitable for me.

I ended up having to tell her that replicating her life was not what I had in mind for myself at all, and that after a brief romance all I saw was her daily grind of sacrifice in which everything she did was focused towards her husband and two children. I regarded my life to be filled with considerably more passion, even though I wasn't sharing it with a man.

It might seem a bit harsh to have pointed this out, but I felt that negating the value of my life as a single woman like that was a huge insult which needed to be addressed.

- Whenever you consider you are on the receiving end of treatment that you are being subjected to only because you are single, ask for this to stop. While on a business trip to Milan, Jemma went down to dinner by herself in her hotel and was directed to a table in a corner of the restaurant, segregated from the other businesspeople and couples. She remarked in a very loud voice that she wasn't happy with this positioning and hoped that the maître d' wasn't discriminating against her just because she was a woman dining by herself. Her forthrightness attracted many positive comments and some applause from fellow diners who commented that a single man would not have been treated in the same way. If other people act in ways that are offensive or unkind to us on the basis of our being single, then we each have a responsibility to speak out as we would if this were done because of our colour, creed or age. If more of us did this, then this kind of sexual discrimination would be weeded out.

Perhaps, like me, you are appalled by the media's – and by association, society's – seeming obsession with the miserable, dysfunctional side of life? By television shows that celebrate abusive behaviour, and which parade all sorts of unhappy individuals on our screens? Then I urge you to do what you can to replace this negativity with an optimistic approach and compelling lifestyle. As Ralph Waldo Emerson once said: 'Be the change you want to see in the world.'

Demonstrate, by every thought, word and deed, that you are extending the boundaries of your life, even if other people are content to place enormous limitations on theirs. If you put your mind to it you could be happy with your life exactly as it is – right now. It's just a case of changing how and what you think – as you are about to find out.

3

Change Your Mind, Transform Your Experiences

'People everywhere enjoy believing things that they know are not true. It spares them the ordeal of thinking for themselves and taking responsibility for what they know.'

Brooks Atkinson (1894–1984), *Once Around the Sun*

Maria had what she considered to be a secure job and comfortable relationship. Neither of these situations set her pulse racing, but there seemed no good reason to change anything. One day, out of the blue, her company announced that – in the wake of the recent merger with another organisation – there were to be large-scale redundancies and Maria was to be one of the casualties. At their regular monthly get-together, Maria's girlfriends commented on how terrible she must feel at losing her job like that. Maria, who had developed a spiritual perspective on life, just shrugged and said, 'Perhaps.'

While looking for suitable employment, Maria was offered some lucrative temporary work that paid her an hourly rate considerably higher than she had been earning before. At their next meeting, her friends all said they were delighted for her and told Maria how lucky she was, but the young woman just smiled enigmatically and replied, 'Perhaps.'

Shortly afterwards, Maria's long-term boyfriend announced that he didn't think their relationship was going anywhere and broke it off. She subsequently discovered through a mutual friend that he had been seeing someone else behind her back for months. Maria's mates were scathing in their criticism of the cheater and said she was fortunate to be rid of him. 'Perhaps,' was all Maria would offer on the subject.

Less than six months after her professional and personal life had been turned upside down, Maria received a call from the agency which had been providing her with temporary work. One of their clients was so impressed with her that they wanted to offer Maria a permanent position – in their Paris office. With no emotional ties to hold her back, and a wonderful opportunity to shift her life out of its previously humdrum existence, Maria immediately said, 'Yes!'

This is a modern spin on an ancient Chinese Taoist story highlighting how, as the context around which your experiences are framed changes, so too does the meaning that you ascribe to those experiences. By not jumping to conclusions about the events that happen in your life, you train yourself to be open-minded as to what they might mean for you in the future. Because, as most of us know if we think about it, what seems like a tragedy when it occurs can be a blessing in disguise, or even something to laugh about with the benefit of hindsight.

Deferring judgement until you have more facts at your disposal reminds me of a recent recruitment advertisement for the UK's Metropolitan Police Force at a time when they were being heavily criticised for alleged institutionalised racism. Presented was a picture of a white, uniformed police officer running behind a sportswear-attired black man. Viewers were prompted into considering the assumptions they came to when looking at this scenario. Then a second, wider image was produced, in which a white youth was introduced into the picture. This immediately changed the context of the original scene and it became clear that this was not a case of a white policeman chasing a black criminal, but of two policemen – one an Afro-Caribbean undercover officer – trying to catch a young delinquent.

These stories are consistent with wisdom passed down through the ages, which suggests that we see things according to entrenched beliefs, expectations and assumptions. These frequently distort not only how we see the world but also the meaning of the experiences we have. Such a message is inherent in the following quotes:

'Men are disturbed not by things but by the views which they take of them.'
Epictetus (AD 55–135)

'As a man is, so he sees.'
William Blake (1757–1827)

'Men who are out of humour with themselves often see their own condition reflected in the world outside them and everything seems amiss because it is not well with themselves.'
James Anthony Froude (1818–94)

'Most folks are as happy as they make their minds up to be.'
Abraham Lincoln (1809–65)

What has attitude – and more specifically the beliefs, assumptions and expectations you have amassed over the years – got to do with being single? One of the downsides of not having a full-time partner is that you have more time to think because you generally get to spend more time by yourself. This is not particularly helpful if your thought processes have a tendency to be more negative than positive. Therefore this chapter is dedicated to helping you to enhance your current perspective on being single by:

- Encouraging you to challenge your current mode of seeing things, in order to recognise unhelpful assumptions, beliefs and behaviours.
- Making you more aware of the inner dialogue which contributes towards biased thinking.
- Helping you reframe your experiences so that you can more readily see the benefits, not the disadvantages, of your current or future situation.
- Assisting you in discovering your current motivational style in order to check that it is not disempowering you or delaying your attempts at action.

Then, and only then, will you be in the best possible position to harness the inner resources you need to change your life for the better and regard being single as a wonderful opportunity filled with untold potential, rather than a situation to be avoided and feared.

The main reason why people find it so difficult to effect long-lasting change is because they haven't addressed the subject of how and what they think. As the quote at the top of this chapter implies, this appears to offer the line of least resistance, whereas in actual fact we attract more pain and unhappiness into our lives because we tend to be more fixated on what we don't want rather than on what we do. According to esoteric writers and those working in the field of personal development, whatever we focus our attention on we'll attract into our lives at some time or another – because intention is a powerful force, be it something we want to happen or something we do not. How many times have you said to yourself, 'I knew that was going to happen'? about something you have fixated on trying to avoid?

In the same way that taking on a new job will involve honing and refining your existing skills, if you want to successfully handle changing circumstances you have to ask yourself whether your existing thought processes are best suited to them. In short, you need to learn how to think more effectively. Sadly, few of us are exposed throughout our life and education to information on how to do this. We are not taught as part of our life skills to make an implicit connection between our thoughts, moods and behaviour. Instead of dealing with the source of our problems – our thoughts – we focus solely on our dysfunctional behaviour in order to mitigate or eliminate the effects. But this is like taking a pill to alleviate a pain. The pain will go away, temporarily, but unless you address why you got it in the first place, and understand what message your body is trying to convey to you, then it will keep on recurring. Is it any wonder we get so dispirited by our tendency to fail to live in a more empowered way despite our efforts to change our behaviour?

Because we in the West are so brainwashed into thinking we can buy ourselves a 'quick fix' involving the least amount of cerebral effort, one of the favourite escape routes we think we have when coming to terms with change is to try and modify the external environment. Yet the most important thing to remember when you want to transform your life, in whatever area – relationships, career, self-image – is that the primary resources you need to draw on are *internal*. When you change the way you think, your external environment changes to support those new beliefs – not the other way around. One such example of 'putting the cart before the horse' involves those people I refer to as 'cosmetic surgery junkies'; individuals who have repeated face lifts, liposuction and breast augmentation in order to try and feel better about themselves.

As a magazine beauty writer for many years I was frequently stunned by the extent to which many quite attractive people would spend a small fortune in an attempt to be happy within themselves. It never seemed to work – which is why, time and again, these people spent their adult lives constantly subjecting their faces and bodies to invasive surgery. Their perception of themselves had nothing to do with what they looked like, but everything to do with how they felt about themselves – their self-esteem. Despite the best efforts of some very gifted surgeons (and, of course, some 'cowboys' – there is always a risk with these kinds of procedures) these cosmetic surgery junkies would look in the mirror and only see the plain, ugly, oversized or unsexy individual they had always thought themselves to be. And in many cases it was their belief in their lack of physical attractiveness that caused them to repel the very person they were trying to attract – a potential life partner.

Because human beings are always looking for ways in which to prove their beliefs to be right, we subconsciously engage in behaviour which will support our negative impression of ourselves. Hence a woman who has spent a fortune on plastic surgery will regard any rejection by a man to be further proof that she is unappealing to men in general. She will disregard the fact that this particular individual may a) not be looking for a relationship right now, b) find her obsession with physical appearance to be a turn-off, c) be attracted to women who exhibit a high measure of self-esteem, regardless of what they look like, or d) not 'click' with her for any number of other reasons.

It may seem strange to focus on learning how and what to think, since this skill is largely neglected in the West. But let's look for a moment at how neglecting to hone and refine these inner resources can have such a debilitating effect on your life. Aside from writing books and articles on self-help issues, I am also a life coach, which means that clients pay me to support, motivate and guide them from where they are currently in their lives to where they want to be. In short, I help people realise their golden vision for their lives. With my help and encouragement one of my clients – Terry – had successfully shifted from being an unhappy employee to setting up his own consultancy business. In order to attract new clients he wrote a very compelling mailshot and arranged for a local business network to distribute these to potential customers. As you may already be aware, this kind of marketing approach requires some follow-up in order to capitalise on the mailing activity. You just can't expect people to come knocking on your door on the basis of a mail out, regardless of how compelling your product or service is. Terry had ended his letter with the promise that he would ring the recipient's office within a week to discuss how he could tailor his services to their needs. The problem was, like many of us, Terry suffered from 'phone fear'. He was paralysed by the thought of ringing up these prospects and possibly have them be rude to him.

When we explored this fear a little more, it emerged that what was really at the core of Terry's phobia was his belief that he was no good at making sales calls. This was not an unreasonable belief, given that he'd had a number of experiences in the past in which – according to his own description – he had 'messed things up'. Because of his lack of confidence when talking on the telephone to people that he had never met, Terry had a tendency to babble. He would then take too long to get to the point of the conversation and, even if he did get the listener interested in what he had to say, he usually failed to 'close the sale'. However, as I pointed out to him, the fact was Terry had never been taught how to make an effective sales call. Like most of us, he gave himself a hard time about this lack of natural ability, for some reason expecting that he should be able to do this and be successful at it. Because of this unrealistic expectation, Terry had actually never done anything practical about learning this skill.

This is analogous to the common tendency to self-flagellate over our inability to cope with changing circumstances, while failing to recognise that we may need to amend or even eliminate existing beliefs, assumptions, expectations and behaviour – in short, to learn to think in a different way. This includes re-evaluating our perceptions of how we think life is and examining how powerfully this accumulated understanding – erroneous or otherwise – affects our emotional, behavioural and physiological responses to our experiences. In Terry's case, all it took was a quick call to book himself on a two-day sales training programme. At the end of this course he had learned how to prepare himself before he made sales calls, how to anticipate and overcome objections, and the different ways in which to encourage the prospective client to invite Terry into the company to discuss how his service could improve their bottom-line.

Ask yourself this: Is your thought life as healthy and as empowering as it could be? If so, then one would assume that you are completely happy and fulfilled in your life. If that's not the case, then perhaps it's time to examine more closely *what* you think, particularly about being a single woman in today's society, and how you might avoid taking on unhelpful assumptions, beliefs and behaviour patterns in the future.

How do you think?

One of the more extreme forms of negative thinking that cognitive therapists have identified is what's been termed 'learned helplessness'. This is a particularly biased way of thinking in which you set yourself up as a victim of life rather than as someone who is in control of her destiny. Hence the tendency to cling on to any relationship, no matter how dysfunctional, because of the erroneous belief that you cannot cope without a man.

Learned helplessness has three components in which problems are considered to be permanent, pervasive and personal. In the context of being single, this translates into the following kind of thoughts: 'I am never going to find anyone who will love me ever again.' (permanent); 'My whole life is a mess, I can't get anything right.' (pervasive); 'Everyone else can find themselves a partner – what's the matter with me?' (personal).

Just consider for a moment how thinking like this sets up a self-fulfilling prophecy of unhappiness in line with our equation that thoughts determine moods which in turn determine behaviour which thereafter affects the way other people relate to us. By eclipsing the glimmer of hope that normal, rational thinking predisposes us to, the above example of learned helplessness causes us to feel apathetic about our future, which incapacitates us against taking any form of action that will improve our situation. After a while even your closest friends get frustrated when you seem unwilling to help yourself; such as always saying you're too tired or fed up to get dressed up and join them for a night out. People start to avoid you because, frankly, you're not much fun to be around. You're urged to 'snap out of it' but don't seem to have the physical energy to drag yourself out of the pit of despair into which you've sunk. You are then caught up in a vicious circle whereby your thought life and external environment impact detrimentally on each other. If you're not careful, you could quickly and easily become clinically depressed.

The central tenet of cognitive therapy, from which the exercises in this chapter have been developed, is that it is our perception of an event, and not the experience itself, which powerfully affects our emotional, behavioural and physiological responses to it. Thoughts precede emotional responses, and therefore in order to change dysfunctional patterns you need to take control of what you think. The moment you begin to view things that happen to you in a different light (not necessarily positive, since negative and neutral perspectives can also be valuable, according to the specific circumstances), even minor changes in this area can lead to a change in your mood, behaviour, physical reactions and life situation.

Personal narrative

Before you begin the exercises in this chapter and work your way through the rest of the book I urge you to write a brief relationship autobiography in your journal. This will help you identify more readily how, over time, your thoughts about certain experiences do in fact change – sometimes quite significantly – and that in fact you choose to think in a particular way, even if you're not always conscious of it. Like a self-exploring scientist this activity encourages you to examine some of your long-held beliefs, assumptions, expectations and behaviour and is an important first step in amassing evidence for and against their current usefulness in your life. Apart from offering an opportunity for self-reflection, setting out your personal narrative in this way will highlight the extent to which you have reinvented yourself in the past and reveal the opinions you have about yourself and the world in general which may no longer be serving you well.

I know that many people avoid engaging interactively with self-help books, believing that they can get what they need just from reading the text. I used to be one of them. But would you consider yourself likely to become proficient at riding at bicycle or driving a car simply by reading a manual on how to do so? Whether you are embracing a new skill, or adapting an existing one, please don't underestimate the value of participation. Simply reading this chapter – and doing nothing else – will give you an intellectual appreciation of how to make significant and life-empowering changes to your life. But in order to integrate these extremely important insights so that you bring about a funda-mental transformation quickly and effectively, it is essential to experience them.

It's up to you. If you really want to change your life for the better and become happier and more fulfilled than perhaps you've ever been in the past, then I urge you now to find time when you will be undisturbed for up to an hour. A time when you feel excited at the prospect of achieving a satisfying single life – even if this is only desired temporarily, while you develop yourself for the kind of relationship you have always dreamed of – and are prepared to devote the time and energy necessary to the following exercises.

Your first step is to begin writing your personal narrative – an overview of all the relationships you have had during your lifetime, including those with your parents, siblings, other significant relatives or carers, very close friends and all your lovers. If you prefer, write this up as a chart by taking a roll of plain lining paper or the reverse side of a roll of wallpaper and, starting at the top-left hand corner and working your way to the right, outline all your relationships in chronological order. Then, under each name write a paragraph about the following:

- The key assumptions you made about this relationship in terms of how you expected yourself and the other person to behave.
- What expectations you held as to the nature of this relationship, present and future – for example, who held the balance of power, and how did you expect that to change, if at all?

- Your beliefs at the time about this relationship – its significance, what it highlighted about your past view of yourself, the other person, and relationships in general.
- The most prevalent moods associated with it – was this a relationship in which you were predominantly happy or sad?
- An example of one or more typical patterns of behaviour you engaged in while you were in this relationship – did you find yourself acting in a needy way? Or especially confidently?

Once you have completed these five paragraphs related to each of the relationships in your journal or on your chart, ask yourself: How does the story you told yourself at the time differ from the way you see things now? If I was writing about my relationship with Stewart, as outlined in Chapter One, my old story would be very different from my new story or the way I view the significance of this relationship today. For example, I believed then that this man was the Great Love of My Life and that we would spend the rest of our lives together. With the benefit of hindsight I have amended that belief, so that while Stewart is still viewed as a significant catalyst in my personal growth and development, I no longer consider him to be a major love that I have lost. If anything, he has moved me on tremendously towards being the kind of self-confident, independent, positive woman I have always known I could be.

What I am directing you towards in this chapter are ways in which you can empower yourself with new beliefs about your present and future happiness based on assessing the current validity of those that you have carried with you up to now. By learning these lessons you will hopefully avoid 'repeat offending' with all the pain and sadness it involves. Simply keep this journal entry or chart where you can refer to it easily as you work your way through other exercises in this book. It contains the seeds of your future personal growth and development.

Exercise: singles thought life

You can use the following techniques for any kind of change you wish to bring about. However, in the context of this book we are going to concentrate on moving you towards acceptance of living for yourself, by yourself, and achieving the life you have always wanted before you even think about inviting another person to share it with you.

I'd like you to complete the following sentence in at least twenty-five different ways by considering what 'being single' means to you at present, regardless of where your assumptions may have come from. Try not to think too hard about this exercise. The most ingrained and hence hard-to-shift attitudes are those which spring to mind most easily. Complete this sentence as quickly as you can, without judging or censoring what you put down.

Being single means..

Contained within the twenty-five sentences you have just written are your core beliefs about what it means to be single. Now re-read them as objectively as you can, assessing what they say about how you see yourself and the world around you. How many of these statements are positive, how many are negative? Do you regard your current life stage as being crammed full of opportunities to be explored, or as something to be feared and therefore avoided at all costs? Make a mental note of whether, according to your current perspective, your life without a partner is filled with lack or potential.

Now we are going to examine the extent to which your beliefs are, in fact, one hundred per cent true all of the time. And whether, by adhering to them rigidly throughout your life, they are serving you well. As you now recognise from the relationship autobiography you prepared in the previous exercise, the meaning you ascribe to an historic episode in your life changes as your experience unfolds. For example, I recently met a man at a wine tasting function whom, within five minutes, I had decided I didn't like. I was there with a friend of his, but he made no immediate effort to introduce himself and responded, to what I considered to be a harmless comment of mine, somewhat aggressively. On face value he did not seem like the kind of person whose company I would enjoy. However, being aware of the importance of practising what I preach I decided to suspend my judgement on this man. When my inner voice leapt to the conclusion, 'He obviously doesn't like you much', like Maria in the opening story I chose to respond with the neutral, 'Perhaps'.

During the evening I watched closely as this man communicated with others. It turned out he took the same irascible stance with everyone in the group, regardless of how long he had known them. I also noticed he had a rather appealing, sarcastic sense of humour, not unlike my own. I chose not to take offence at his sharp manner and do what I would normally do (avoid his company), but to engage him in conversation instead. Once the evening got underway and the wine tasting was in full flow we began a delightful and often amusing dialogue. By the time we got round to saying our goodnights, I had decided he was rather fun to be around and looked forward to meeting him again.

This brief episode serves to illustrate how several common, long-held beliefs can be confounded – if you are prepared to defer making assumptions. The first erroneous belief is that we are equipped to make an accurate assessment of a person within the first few minutes of meeting them. Having decided that someone is rude, boring or whatever else, we mentally limit the opportunities we might have for really getting to know them. The second belief-buster is that if someone is aggressive or sharp with you, it is personal, and they are indicating they dislike you in some way. I'm sure you've also met people who, though first appearing rude or unpleasant, turn out to be desperately shy or have difficulty interacting with others. This has nothing to do with *you*, and everything to do with *them*.

Taking each of the twenty-five statements that you have written down regarding what being single means to you, I would like you to act like a scientist exploring a hypothesis rather than a fact. This involves looking for evidence to support or reject each of your assertions. For example, one of the ways in which women complete the above sentence is by insinuating that being single involves being less happy than being in a relationship. If we turn that assumption on its head, what we are saying is that people are happier when in relationships. But is this really true at a time when divorce statistics are soaring? If people were always that happy in their relationships would they be splitting up at such a rate? Try objectively reviewing the relationships of some of your friends. Are they always – or even intermittently – blissful? I can think of at least half a dozen friends who are married or seriously involved with guys and who are having major relationship problems. Right now they are pretty miserable. In my own experience some of my most unhappy and painful experiences have been while I was in relationships. They are not always a bed of roses.

For each of your statements, ask yourself if there is another way of seeing things. What other perspective might you take? Instead of equating being alone as leading a lonely life, you might think of it as offering total freedom of choice. Similarly, living by yourself has very positive connotations when you consider that it also means having the space in which to express yourself without worrying in case your plans encroach on anyone else. As Maria found, her new single status meant that she could take the job offer in Paris without concerning herself as to whether it would upset her boyfriend.

Doubting what you have long-since believed is a very empowering way of relating to the world, which is why René Descartes (1596–1650), considered the father of modern philosophy, advised:

'If you would be a real seeker after truth, it is necessary that at least once in your life you doubt, as far as possible, all things.'

And one of poet Robert Browning's (1812–89) mottoes was:

'Who knows most, doubts most.'

By questioning the validity of what you believe as being relevant to all circumstances and in all cases, you are preparing yourself for one of the most powerful, therapeutic tools used to help permanently change dysfunctional behaviour – reframing.

But before we look at how reframing can help you embrace being single more enthusiastically, let's examine exactly where some of your unhelpful assumptions, beliefs and hence thoughts, moods and behaviour patterns originated from. For someone who thinks she is in control of her own mind, you might be surprised to discover the extent to which your inner dialogue is influenced by others.

Your inner dialogue

As was pointed out earlier, external influences – whether from television, newspapers and magazines or other people – have a powerful effect on our thoughts. Researchers constantly discover that people's fears of the risk of being mugged, raped, murdered or dying in a plane crash – the chances of which are extremely small – are seriously skewed. This is because, day after day, we pick up or hear stories of doom and gloom that present the world as a much more dangerous place than it actually is for the vast majority of us. Be aware from now on of the messages you absorb from the world around you, particularly in relation to being single. Take a critical look at features about single life in the media you subject yourself to. Listen to your own and other people's language when talking about being single. Ironically, I was guilty of this myself when I innocently asked one of my interviewees how she had come to terms with being single. Della, twice divorced with a thirteen-year gap between marriages, answered me this way:

> Frankly, I get rather annoyed at questions like that. I don't view my life as having to come to terms with anything since this implies that I have lost something or don't have what I want. In point of fact my professional and personal lives are

quite fulfilling, exciting and an awful lot of fun. Being in a relationship is not the beginning and end of my world, although one or two of my relationhips have played a significant part at a particular stage in my life. I've always pretty much done what I've wanted to do and never thought I should rush off and marry somebody to make myself a worthwhile person, because I take the view that I'm pretty complete without having to attach myself to a man.

As you look through your relationship history again, check for clues about the nature of your inner dialogue and consider where these biased views may have come from. Was it covertly from your mother who insinuated that if you weren't married by the age of twenty-five then you'd never find a nice man to settle down with and have children? Perhaps your views of being single were influenced subconsciously by pitying an aunt who had never married and seemed to live a very lonely and sad existence. Or from noticing that in your circle any woman who suddenly found herself without a partner was excluded from events and therefore didn't just lose her man, but her social life too?

Words to watch out for while exploring these mental models are: 'should', 'must', 'ought', 'have to', 'always', 'never' and 'nobody' (as in 'Nobody ever makes an effort to befriend me – I always have to make the first move.'). Wherever possible allow a light bulb to go off whenever you hear these words – spoken by yourself or someone else – and assess the extent to which such over-generalising, catastrophising, exaggerative, 'black and white' language masks a core belief that is both erroneous and unhealthy.

Remember that assumptions give birth to expectations which can turn into some pretty unfortunate, self-fulfilling prophecies. Spiritual philosophies such as Buddhism and Taoism teach that freedom from suffering comes only when we are prepared to give up our attachment to specific outcomes. That is, our expectations of how things should be. However, this is a very challenging principle for human beings to embrace in our everyday lives. So, if you insist on hanging on for dear life to your assumptions and expectations, at least make them positive ones: wherever possible, expect to succeed, expect to be happy. Expectations are powerful determinants of behaviour as the following two historical anecdotes illustrate:

No athlete had run a sub-four-minute mile before the UK's Roger Bannister did so in 1954. Not long after his achievement had been broadcast to the world, more and more runners began to equal, and then break, that record. It wasn't that the physical prowess or preparation of these athletes had fundamentally changed, just that they now believed such a speed was possible and this fuelled the expectation that they could do likewise. After all, there was nothing superhuman about Bannister.

Similarly, in 1961, when the then US President, John F. Kennedy, announced that the United States of America would put a man on the moon before the end of the decade, this public declaration encouraged those working on the space programme to make it a reality. And indeed it became so in July 1969, when the USA's Neil Armstrong and Buzz Aldrin walked on the moon's surface.

Take another look over your journal notes – those containing your relationship autobiography, your statements about what being single means to you and your current inner dialogue and its influences – and reconsider what expectations you have about your life as a single woman. If these are negative, determine to confound them. The following technique demonstrates how:

Reframing your experiences

In the way that the same picture would look different if you surrounded it with an ornate, gold border as opposed to a functional, plain black one, your experiences will take on a different meaning depending on the various beliefs you frame them with. This involves consciously choosing a more therapeutic response to life events rather than being saddled with an outmoded set of self-limiting beliefs. This is not to say that your beliefs, assumptions and behaviour haven't served you well in the past, but rather that new circumstances may now require a more appropriate set of responses, though it's not wise to assume that you will automatically be able to access or organise these new behavioural patterns without going through some kind of learning process.

Before you begin to learn anything at all, it's an important first step to identify what your objective is. What is it you want to achieve? What do you need in order to live a life of happiness and fulfilment, irrespective of whether or not you have a partner? Sometimes it's very difficult to know exactly what you want, which is why visualising is such a valuable technique to use.

Nine steps you need to take to help you create a compelling picture in your mind of your future life:

1. Settle yourself down in your favourite place either indoors or outside. Somewhere quiet and warm where you won't be disturbed for at least half an hour. Choose a time when you feel neither tired nor over-energised, but calm and centred both mentally and physically. Make sure that whatever position you select – either lying down or sitting in a chair – you are comfortable. Adjust yourself as much as you need to before you begin this visualisation exercise.

2. Close your eyes and begin focusing on your breathing. Breathe slowly and deeply in and out through your nose. Feel any mental or physical tension draining away with each out breath. Be aware of your thoughts, but don't dwell on them. Allow them to drift through your mind like a piece of driftwood floating down a stream.

3. When you feel mentally and physically relaxed, bring to mind all the things that are important to you which you get from someone else, or which you feel you do not have currently but admire in others: such as security, love, comfort, total confidence, reassurance, high self-esteem, a sense of purpose etc. Make your list as long as you like. Just keep thinking of everything you need for your life to be as joyful and fulfilled as possible. Do not censor or judge these thoughts – allow your

subconscious to communicate with you without any self-sabotaging mechanisms getting in the way.

4. Now ask yourself: How will you know when you have each of these attributes? What would it be like to feel totally secure, loved or confident? Ask your subconscious mind what evidence you would need to convince yourself that you are living a life that is truly fulfilled. Become aware of how this knowledge comes to you – as words, pictures, sounds, fragrances or sensations in a particular part of your body.

5. Imagine that your whole self has become magnetised and is drawing all these attributes towards you. Merge with them in whatever way seems appropriate to you – perhaps as colours that suffuse your body, or pictures that you assemble in a mental photograph album. Take your time over this to ensure each of these desirable characteristics becomes securely integrated into your entire being.

6. Concentrate once more on your breathing as you revisit each of these positive characteristics, focusing on how this feels and exactly where in your body these sensations emanate from.

7. When you are confident that you have securely anchored the sensations related to all the factors that contribute to your living the most joyful and fulfilled life you can possibly imagine, open your eyes. Stretch your arms and legs and take a sip or two of water to ground yourself in the present.

8. Take a moment to reflect on this visualisation experience, then make a note in your journal of all the attitudes, beliefs and responses that you have just mentally embraced in order to achieve a more positive, independent, self-confident version of yourself.

9. Get into the habit, at least every morning and evening, of re-experiencing the sensations you felt or the images that came to you during your visualisation. Make this a ritual that you commit to, one in which you are strengthening the inner resources that will equip you to better deal with present and future experiences.

The more often you reflect on what you discovered during your visualisation the easier you will find it to be aware of the limiting beliefs and behaviour that are shackling you to old ways of thinking and being. Don't give yourself a hard time if you find yourself slipping back into habitual behaviour. Of course, you will – it's like preferring to put on a pair of comfortable shoes that you're hardly aware of wearing rather than subjecting yourself to breaking in brand new ones that pinch with every step. It's much more tempting to stick with the old pair – until it starts to rain and your feet begin to get wet. Similarly, you could stick to your current behaviour and 'make do' with the life you are leading now. But if you really want to embrace the benefits of your single status without constantly regretting not having a man in your life, then you need to take small incremental steps towards changing the way you think and behave.

I came upon the following wonderfully inspiring example of choosing empowering thoughts when I was writing my book, *Working from the Heart*, about finding the work you love and loving the work you do. It's about the relationship a group of young men, working at the Pike Place Fish Company in Seattle, have with each other, their employer, their customers and their work, and is a perfect example of reframing.

Selling fish day in day out isn't everyone's idea of a great job. It involves getting up very early in the morning, in all weathers, weighing fish, and taking money from an increasingly discerning general public. Boring, huh? Well that's one way of looking at it. An alternative way to frame this work is to think of it as fun. And that's exactly what's on the menu for the Pike Place employees and their customers. Each of these guys chooses to put a positive spin on his work and how he approaches it. They make the time and effort to really listen and interact with each and every customer – not treat them as if they were unimportant, as so many salespeople do nowadays. They crack jokes, invite customers behind the counter to see how well they can catch fish and generally have such a good time that it's common for a crowd to gather just to listen to their banter. Because of this enlightened approach to their work, the Pike Place Fish Company philosophy has been captured on a training video so that other organisations and their staff can benefit from taking a similar attitude. In this video, one of the workers captures the mood of reframing when he points out that he could wake up each morning and think what a lousy job he's doing and, with that attitude make his own, his colleagues' and his customers' lives a misery. However, he chooses not to. Given the fact that this is the only job he currently has, he elects to view this as constructively as possible. And in return he enjoys a positive work experience.

Once you have formulated a compelling outcome for your life, and have identified the kinds of attitudes and behaviour you need to embrace in order to make that vision a reality, then it's pretty much a case of adhering to the gospel according to Nike: 'Just do it.' Remember the words of Eleanor Roosevelt: 'Anyone can conquer fear by doing the things (s)he fears to do, provided (s)he keeps doing them until (s)he gets a record of successful experiences behind her/him.'

Be alert in your daily life, instead of sleepwalking as most of us do. Pay attention to your inner dialogue, the assumptions you habitually make, and the unhelpful habits that you've got into. Take a risk. Reinvent yourself. Only by constant reframing can you acquire the sort of successful experiences that produce evidence that a new, more joyful life is possible for you – with or without a partner. Whatever happens to you, and before you jump to a conclusion about it, ask yourself: 'What other perspective can I take about this event?'

One of the key differences I discovered between women who are contentedly single and those who are not is, ironically, that the former group don't view their relationship status as being a fundamental factor in their self-image. Della put it this way:

I don't think of myself as being either single or married but just 'me'. That's why, when I ask someone to mail me some information and they inquire if I'm a Miss or a Mrs I say, 'What's that got to do with anything?' Because to me it's irrelevant whether I'm married or not.

Erin takes this perspective:

I didn't make up my mind to be single, just as I never made up my mind not to get married or not have children. I think it's too easy to stereotype and people have some unfortunate labels for what they define as a single person – such as being left on the shelf and ending up an old maid. But I don't think about being single. I just have a life.

While forty-year-old Harriet, an accountant working for a charity, who has never been married, adds:

Status is just what other people say about you so they can place you in some neat little box. Well, I'm not interested in allowing other people to confine my life in this way. I choose not to live within boundaries. And I'm more interested in what I have to tell myself. That's why I wake up each morning deliberately focusing on the good things that happen and all the beauty in the world. And it's a funny thing, you know? So many more good and beautiful things happen to me compared with most other people.

These women know that the only way in which they can always get what they want is to secure it from the one person they can always count on – themselves. Part of this self-supporting process involves constantly reminding themselves of the life outcomes they want. They habitually talk to themselves in a positive way, and you can learn to do this too by repeating, every day, a set of specifically worded affirmations – short statements focusing on the outcome you have chosen for yourself and the various ways in which you intend to fulfil it.

I always believe it's best if you write your own affirmations, rather than slavishly repeat ones that you read in a book, no matter how appealing they seem. This is because you need to make them unique to you and your specific circumstances. However, there are six key features of a well-formed affirmation which you should incorporate when writing your affirmations. Ideally they:

1. Are written in the first person and the present tense.
2. Imply that you are moving from where you are to where you want to be, e.g. 'I am becoming...'
3. Are positive and uplifting – like a rousing speech, they galvanise you into taking action.
4. Are very specific, dealing with whatever limiting beliefs or behaviour patterns you currently want to change.
5. Use words that prompt a visual response – they paint pictures in your head.
6. Get right to the heart of what it is you want to achieve for your life – they are about the desires of your soul, not the logical assessment of your mind.

Here are some examples that might inspire you:

- I am becoming the most loving, supportive, nurturing friend to myself.
- I am learning to love my life exactly as it is – no matter whether I have a companion on the journey or not.
- I am opening myself up to seeing life as full of wonderful opportunities, just waiting for me to savour them.
- I am beginning to recognise there is no one way of viewing my reality, but a whole range of alternative perspectives. I love having so much choice.
- Every day in every way I am strengthening my belief that my life is glorious – exactly as it is.
- My life is like a surprise gift, filled to the brim with wonderful treasures for me to explore and enjoy as, and when, I choose.
- I am becoming less dependent on others for my sense of self-esteem and self-worth.

- I am committed to my goal of living life to the fullest, always discovering joy and pleasure in every experience.

In addition, twelve of my favourite statements of intent are included at the end of this chapter.

Now try writing your own affirmations, remembering to repeat them to yourself every morning as you wake up and every evening before you settle down to sleep. Psychologists estimate that it takes twenty-eight days to embed a new belief in your mind. The analogy I like to use is that of walking across a field of knee-high grass. On the first day, there is no obvious route, so you wade through the meadow in the direction of your goal. The next day, there is still no clear path across the field, because the grass has sprung back up. But, if you continue taking the same route every day, eventually a track is created until, a month after you first began, you no longer have to think about where you are going – a clearly defined passageway is right in front of you. Similarly, the neurological pathways that are created with each thought you have are strengthened with every repetition of your affirmations.

So far, we have looked at the direct link between your thoughts, moods and behaviour. Hopefully by now you will have completed your relationship autobiography and the other exercises outlined, and have become more aware of the various ways in which you sabotage your happiness by holding on to outmoded beliefs. You will have begun to recognise the inner dialogue – and the influences from others – that does not support your new, empowered way of looking at the world, and will have taken some steps to re-frame your perspectives. And you will have started to take some action through daily repetition of positive affirmations in order to create the life you truly want for yourself.

I'd like to round up this chapter by bringing your attention to the various ways in which we self-sabotage. Which of these behaviours do you recognise in yourself prior to taking some form of action, whether it be starting a new diet, joining a new social circle or applying for another job?

- Do you fixate on what you don't want rather than what you do, as in 'I don't want to be fat anymore', 'I don't want to be lonely' or 'I hate my work so much I need to look for another job'? If you focus your thoughts on desires like these, your mind is constantly receiving messages about being fat, lonely and hating work. These are the key words that are being acted upon. Hence the old maxim, 'Be careful what you wish for – it may come true.'

- Do you have a tendency to command yourself to do things in a dictatorial manner, such as 'I must lose weight', 'I have to force myself to go out tonight' or 'I should do something about updating my CV'? Imagine how you would feel if someone else was to order you around like that? Would you feel like co-operating? What do you think your subconscious self feels like when it receives this kind of communication?

- When you visualise the future do you mentally fast-forward only as far as what you're going to do, not what it will be like when you have done it? As you discovered in the earlier visualisation exercise, an important factor in motivating yourself to make fundamental changes is producing evidence of what it will be like when you have achieved your goal. When you are able realistically to experience the sense of satisfaction and completion that comes from being successfully single then you are bringing the future into the present, thereby compelling the external environment to change to support your new state. Hence, in the above examples, you need to *know* what it will feel like to fit into the clothes you want to wear, to be a popular member of a new group of friends and to enjoy work that is satisfying and rewarding. You have been equipped with the perfect tool in order to do this. It's called your imagination – use it!

- Are you inclined to overwhelm yourself by seeing only the big picture? By focusing so much on the enormity of the task in front of you that you become totally paralysed and find it hard to motivate yourself into any action whatsoever? As the ancient Chinese saying goes, 'Every journey begins with a single step.'

Get into the habit of breaking down your goals into the individual tasks you need to undertake to make them a reality, in the same way that you would cut a 32 oz steak into bite-sized chunks before attempting to eat it. If I sat down and fixated on how much work was involved in writing a book like this, I would probably never get a word written. That's why I write a very detailed synopsis, outlining exactly what I'm going to put in each chapter, the messages I want to get across, and the tools and techniques I'm going to include. Then I produce a timetable for myself in which I set individual deadlines for each of the sections in each of the chapters. Writing 1000–2000 words a day is much easier for me to get my head round than completing a book stretching to 60,000 words. Similarly, achieving the life you want seems both overwhelming and a somewhat nebulous concept until you sit down and specify exactly what it would mean to you to achieve it, and what incremental steps you need to take to make it a reality.

It's not being Pollyanna-ish to believe that every experience you have has some benefit for your growth and development. The trick is to remain open-minded to the belief that there is an alternative perspective to your situation, and to apply some effort, or have a degree of patience, in order to find out what that might be. For example, someone crashed into my car, breaking one of the wing mirrors on a day when I was due to give a talk in London, one week before I was due to visit the US for three months. Not the most positive experience, you might say. But a considerable benefit came out of it.

Having taken my car into the local garage, the owner pointed out that I had a few patches of rust on the driver's door. I hadn't spotted them. He said he would have a word with his contact at the manufacturer's – whom he knew very well – to check whether this was covered under my warranty. This turned out to be the case, and the work was done on the same day that my wing mirror was replaced. The warranty for bodywork on my car had been due to expire before I returned from the US. I doubt I would have noticed that rust in the time left to me in England and therefore I would have had to pay for this work to be done outside of the warranty cover, or allow the bodywork to gradually become more damaged.

There is a raft of benefits from being single that you are probably not aware of right now. By the time you have finished reading this book, hopefully you will be more conscious of them. All you have to do to transform your life for the better is to change your mind about it. As women, we are accused of doing this all the time by men – we might as well use this skill to our advantage.

Now that we have considered the benefits of developing a positive mental attitude generally, let's focus on one area that is of vital importance to your future happiness and wellbeing – that of having an enhanced opinion of yourself. The experiences you have in your life ultimately reflect the quality of your relationship with yourself. If you constantly undervalue yourself, don't be surprised when other people undervalue you. If you deny yourself pleasure, then others will do so too. Alternatively, the moment you start to love yourself wholeheartedly and unconditionally then the universe will be poised to cherish and nurture you in ways you never thought possible. When you turn to the next chapter, be prepared to discover how wonderful it feels to fall in love with the most wonderful person in the world . . . yourself.

General statements of intent

1. I totally accept myself as a wonderful, unique individual, even with all my human limitations and problems.
2. I forgive _____ (your former partner) for leaving me; everything is working out for my highest good, even if I don't recognise that right now.
3. I let go of the past – it no longer exists. I commit to focusing on the gift of life, the present.
4. I always try to do the best I can for myself and others, even though the situation I am in now is challenging.
5. I know that in one, five, ten years from now none of this will

matter to me, even though it doesn't seem that way right now.

6. There is hope in my heart even though I have to remember to keep digging deep to release it.

7. I choose to be at peace with my life, exactly as it is.

8. I know exactly what I need to do to move more quickly into a joyful life. I am learning to trust my intuition.

9. In many ways I know I don't give myself credit for, I'm in control of my destiny.

10. I am worthy of the very best that life has to offer.

11. My ability to look after and nurture myself remains undiminished, even though I feel fearful, angry or alone from time to time.

12. I accept that for every ending there is a beginning, and I embrace that opportunity with all my heart.

4

Love Yourself,
Expand Your Life

'Is life not a thousand times too short for us to bore ourselves?'
Friedrich Nietzsche

Those of us who have a tendency to allow one relationship to immediately follow another often find that we have become so focused on loving someone else that we spend little or no time cherishing ourselves. It isn't surprising that we haven't ever got into the habit of lavishing love on ourselves and feeling okay about it in the first place, considering the messages that we often received as children – when, for example, the implication, from the tone of voice or sneering expression of a parent or primary carer, was that thinking highly of yourself or desiring to put your emotional needs above those of others was, for some reason, unacceptable. I remember vividly an uncle saying to me: 'You really love yourself, don't you?' in a way that made it obvious that this was not what he considered nice people did. That was around the time that I began to care too much about what other people thought of me instead of applauding the fact that I *did* have a high opinion of myself. Ironically, it was only when I started to lavish more love on others than I did on myself that things changed for the worse and my life became an emotional wilderness. But it took me a while to connect the two. The more unhappy my life became, the more I thought that I had to concentrate all my affection externally – on other people. One day I realised that, because life reflects back at us what is going on internally, the reason people kept disappointing me and letting me down was because I was treating myself in exactly that way. I was completely neglecting the one person who deserved my love and attention more than anyone else – me.

Yet I bet you felt uncomfortable reading that last paragraph. Western religion and society in general teaches us that to be considered 'good people' we should ensure we are way down the pecking order when it comes to lavishing love and attention. This message is a distortion of what a spiritual teacher like Jesus Christ meant when he said, 'Love thy neighbour as thyself.' Note, he didn't preach: 'Love thy neighbour more than thyself', but '. . . as thyself', which is just another way of saying you have to know how to love yourself first before you are capable of fully loving anyone else.

Befriend yourself

If you had a friend who was always there for you, who never let you down and supported you no matter what, wouldn't you want to demonstrate how much you loved her? Then why fall short of doing that for yourself? Is it because you have never developed a friendship with yourself? And if not, why not? That's what we're going to focus on in this chapter – the importance of loving yourself and, in so doing, expanding your life in ways which you may not have thought possible.

Following on from the last chapter in which we looked at the importance of attitude, we're now going to consider how you feel about yourself. One of the biggest indicators of a person's level of self-love and self-worth is the extent to which they feel lonely in their own company. That's not to say any one of us would relish being a hermit, but if you cannot cope with a short period of solitude then you have to ask yourself what is going on here. If you really believed yourself to be a fascinating, interesting, stimulating human being – which, of course, you are – then presumably you would have no problem enjoying your own company. And if you don't hold that belief, let's do something to change that right now. Starting with your issues around being lonely.

Five different situations which can be identified as being the most common catalysts for feelings of loneliness

1. Living alone.
2. Finding it challenging to make friends or communicate in a meaningful way with other people.
3. Being geographically distant from your family and/or close friends – perhaps through relocating to another part of the country or world.
4. The isolation caused by temporary physical limitations – such as having a broken leg and being confined to bed, or having no car in a district where there is little or no public transportation.
5. Having no one in the world you feel connected to.

Ask yourself which of these really apply to your situation. You may live alone but do you honestly have *no one* in your life that you can relate to? Thankfully, we live in an age when electronically at least we can connect almost instantly with individuals right across the world. But it's not the quantity of people available to us that mitigates loneliness, but the quality of those interactions. And if you really do consider yourself so disconnected from life as not to have a single soul that you could share a meaningful conversation with, then might not your current situation be the impetus you need to change this?

If you've recently come out of a relationship and are still grieving over that loss – and don't forget it can sometimes take several years to get over a long-term partnership – it is easy to mix up this pain and heartache with what it means to be on your own. It's because of this misunderstanding that we become so desperate to fill the void with another relationship. The false belief goes something like this:

A: I'm not with him any more and it hurts.
B: I feel lonely without him.
Ergo: It hurts when I'm lonely.

Yet the two states of loneliness and grief are quite distinct. The first thing you have to do, which is why this issue was covered in an earlier chapter, is to work your way through your grief. Then, and only then, are you in a position to explore and embrace the wonderful opportunities that the solitude of singleness can offer. Note that I've used the word 'solitude' in that last sentence and not 'loneliness'. I don't consider the two words to be synonymous. For me, and the many happily single women with whom I've discussed this issue, solitude is a deliberate choice. It's about saying, 'Hey, world, I want to spend time by myself to take stock of my life and what's going on inside of me, and to enjoy the things that I love to do without having to compromise my needs by fitting in with someone else.' Loneliness, on the other hand, suggests lack. And whenever we feel our life is lacking in something we experience disappointment or pain.

This is why I urge you not to mix up missing an ex-partner and the loneliness that entails with the kind of life you can expect as a single woman. Frankly, it's up to you how rich or desolate your life is to be – which is why, in this chapter, we also look at ways in which you can enhance your social life. It is important also to balance that sense of community and connection with times when you can enjoy the sort of quiet, nurturing time that women, caught up in the day-to-day demands of relating to their partners, often wish they could have.

But first, let's deal with the inevitable sense of loneliness that is part and parcel of the human condition. When I asked my interviewees how they dealt with loneliness, their responses were fascinating. Here are a few examples:

Erin, who scores highly on what has been termed 'emotional intelligence', says:

> If I feel lonely I address it and say, 'This is what I'm feeling. I feel lonely. I need a hug.' It doesn't mean I need a man in the same way that, sometimes, I fancy a piece of chocolate, but wouldn't think of going out and buying a sweet shop. It's not a good idea to fill your life with a succession of men – suitable or otherwise – just because you occasionally feel lonely. We're all going to feel lonely even when we're in a relationship, because sometimes you may have to be parted from your partner for a time. It's when your sense of loneliness becomes overwhelming that you need to look at what's going on with your own self-esteem issues because when you're that vulnerable, needy and lonely, there's a good chance you'll completely drain a man anyway. They can't fill that gap – only you can do that.

Erin's last point is particularly important to remember with regard to the quality of your future relationships since neediness fuelled by a sense of loneliness will turn a guy who owns himself off, and a dsyfunctional guy on.

Harriet, forty, who has never been married, has got being single down to a fine art:

> I just find life so wonderful I can't get enough of it. There's always something fun to do, much of which doesn't require anyone else there for it to be enjoyable. Being alone doesn't equate to being lonely if you look for all the new things you can learn every day. I paint, I love to go out shopping by myself, which is infinitely preferable to spending half the time trudging round stores that the other person wants to visit. I grow things in my garden and watch the cycle of nature, which helps remind

me how things change, and that winter always turns to spring; I set up daily goals for myself like devouring a certain number of books in a month, and I do things like riding the night buses in London during the summer to enjoy the beauty of the city when it isn't noisy and crowded. All these things make me feel free.

Divorcee Lorna, who has lived by herself for the past three years, travelling abroad three or four times a year, has this perspective:

A sense of adventure is my primary life value and therefore the kind of routine that so many relationships get locked into is anathema to me. My maxim is to be occupied by life, not to be an onlooker. If I had to consider a man in my life I would never have had as many adventures as I have. I booked myself on an inexpensive touring holiday with a mixed crowd, only a few of whom were single, and visited Mayan temples in Mexico. We all got on famously and had a rare old time. I get the cheapest airfare I can to New York and hang out with my girlfriends there. I might take off one weekend and go for a hike in the country.

Who has time to be lonely? I remember reading a quote by Lady Bird Johnson, the former US First Lady, who said: 'Become so wrapped up in something that you forget to be afraid.' I've changed that to: 'Become so wrapped up in life that you forget to be lonely.' If you want to sit around, mope and feel sorry for yourself then that's up to you. But what's that going to achieve? Nothing but a living death. My advice is, if you want to overcome your sense of loneliness, don't sit at home and brood on it, get out – and get busy.

Those of us who have had long-term relationships followed by periods of being single know that it is not your external environment, and who is or is not in it, that determines whether you feel lonely, but your attitude towards your situation. I've known many married women who describe themselves as lonely in their relationships because that's how they feel inside. They've spent so much time and energy giving 150 per cent to their partnership that they've become disconnected from who *they* are, and hence feel disconnected from life. The fact is, you can feel as lonely in the middle of a crowd of people as you can being by yourself. And a sense of being isolated and alone is certainly common when you're in a dysfunctional relationship, one that fails to meet your needs.

Spiritual perspectives

I have found that this internal sense of loneliness can be mitigated by taking a very different perspective on life: a perspective that, while having its roots in spirituality is also finding credence in the realm of science. Spiritual teachers from Buddha to Jesus Christ have taught that we are all intimately connected. Unfortunately, many of us have become indoctrinated by Western orthodox religion which promotes the opposite message – that, being separated from God through original sin, our mission is to become virtuous enough in life to be allowed to reconnect with the Divine in death. I have always been more inclined towards Eastern philosophies which teach that Divine consciousness and human consciousness are made of the same stuff, and that we reside in the Divine just as the Divine resides in us.

Certainly, whether or not you believe in a Divine being, eminent scientists working in the fields of quantum physics, fractal mathematics and chaos theory have done much to validate the philosophical belief that there is an intrinsic relationship between all things. Their postulations have helped overturn the Newtonian view of the universe as one enormous machine, instead portraying it as a cosmic web of infinite vibrational energy. With the discovery of subatomic particles, atoms were no longer regarded as hard, impenetrable 'billiard balls' with distinct and separate boundaries, but as multi-levelled fields of vibrating energy. What we see or experience as 'differences' – such as colour or sound – are simply the effects of such energy fields vibrating at contrasting rates. This also extends to relationships. It has been suggested that the reason why we are attracted to some individuals and repelled by others is to do with matching frequencies and resonances. Think of it in terms of a tuning fork. For example, when such a device, tuned to note A, is sounded near a piano, all the strings that are also tuned to A will resonate while the others will not. This is known as sympathetic vibration.

Similarly, the esoteric concept of a pulsating field known as the 'aura' has recently been validated by eminent scientists from the US to the Far East, only they term it a bioelectromagnetic field. Whatever you wish to call it, the fact is that we are not bounded by our human bodies but extend energetically several feet from it, all the time intermingling with everything around us. This perspective is relevant to the illusion of 'singleness' for two reasons:

1. It demonstrates that our separation from each other is an illusion, and that in fact we cannot be separated from our environment or each other because we are all made from the same seething mass of vibrating energy.
2. It explains how, when you elevate your own vibrational rate to a higher state of consciousness, you begin to attract new, more positive and empowering situations and people into your life.

If you keep these two points in mind, it may help you feel less isolated in your life.

A number of years ago, when I was in Australia, I came across an advertising slogan which stated: 'Life – be in it.' One of the best ways to overturn feelings of loneliness is to focus your attention outwardly, rather than inwardly. The very action of filling your life with things that interest you sparks off a virtuous circle. To become interesting to others you first need to be interested enough in your own happiness to treat every moment as full of potential for learning and experiencing something new. And the more you learn and experience the more you will appreciate that life is far too precious to waste by indulging yourself in feelings of loneliness and boredom.

Here's an invaluable exercise that will help you shake off occasional bouts of loneliness. I'd like you to come up with at least thirty nice things (so you have a full month of activities to start with) that you can do for yourself, by yourself. I know how challenging that can be so I've made a list of suggested pursuits that you can do totally alone or in the company of others. The important thing about each of them, however, is that you do not need to be in a partnership to enjoy them. This list is not exhaustive, nor does it go into any great detail. The idea is that each one of these suggestions will spark off some lateral thinking in you. Be creative, in a way you find both appealing and appropriate:

All alone time

1. Make bath time a nurturing or sensuous experience – use scented candles, essential oils, soothing music.
2. Prepare a dinner party to which only you are invited – cook your favourite food and decorate the table in a way that pleases you.
3. Think of the books you have always wanted to read – and buy or borrow them.
4. Be silent for a whole evening – that is, with no TV, radio or music blaring; make a note of, and intend to act upon, all the creative thoughts that pop into your head.
5. Clear your home of clutter – throw out or recycle items that do not hold any personal meaning or value for you.
6. Buy a bunch of flowers and arrange them beautifully.
7. Go for a walk somewhere remote and really take notice of the colours and textures of your surroundings.
8. Make a compilation tape of your favourite classical or contemporary music to play in your car or on evenings alone.
9. Start writing that novel you've always said is in you – get up an hour or two earlier or retire a little later if you cannot find time during the day.

10. Learn a foreign language through the use of audio tapes, videos, books or recorded TV programmes.
11. Learn a new craft.
12. Paint or draw.
13. Sew a quilt in which the material, colours, textures and patterns each say something about your life so far.
14. Read the Bible or other spiritual work.
15. Write long letters to your friends.
16. Begin your autobiography.
17. Put all your photographs in albums and annotate them.
18. Keep a scrapbook of your life and what's important to you.
19. Read all the columns and reports in the Sunday newspapers that you normally avoid (e.g. sports or financial sections).
20. Surf the Internet.
21. Enter consumer competitions.
22. Write poetry.
23. Plan a party.
24. Sort through your paperwork and set up a personal filing system so that you will never again be unable to lay your hands on your TV licence or car documents.
25. Do crossword puzzles or other, mind-stimulating games.
26. Create an altar decked with items that lift your spirits.
27. Learn to meditate.
28. Start a correspondence course of study.
29. Devise new recipes and have fun tasting your concoctions.
30. Tend your garden.

Sharing with others
1. Volunteer to do charity work.
2. Chart your family history (interviewing family members as appropriate).
3. Join a debating society.
4. Get involved in amateur dramatics.
5. Help out with other people's children.
6. Help out with elderly people.
7. Join a sports team, club or gym.

8. Visit a museum, art gallery, exhibition, historical monument etc.
9. Go to dancing classes.
10. Take an adult education class.
11. Join a wine tasting club.
12. Stimulate an interest in photography.
13. Browse antique or second-hand book stores.
14. Take music lessons.
15. Book a regular health treatment e.g. aromatherapy massage.
16. Join a creative writing group.
17. Get involved in a community project.
18. Sit on a committee.
19. Campaign for a political candidate.
20. Raise funds for a good cause.
21. Contact people you've liked but have lost touch with and catch up on what's been happening in their lives.
22. Join a trade or professional organisation and attend meetings.
23. Join a special interest group.
24. Join your old school association.
25. Explore the religious or spiritual groups in your area.
26. Find a housemate.
27. Join a movie club.
28. Investigate what book readings/discussion groups are on at your local library or bookstore.
29. Go to the movies.
30. Make a point of talking to a complete stranger at least once a day – even if it's just saying, 'Hello, how are you today?'

Just because you are single there is no need to focus solely on activities geared to people who are not in relationships. That way you are labelling yourself unnecessarily and will perhaps think of your social life as only linked to finding a partner, rather than being a fulfilling entity in itself. Whatever you choose to do with your spare time it is important to fill it with pursuits that engross you. In that way you will increase what American psychologist Mihaly Csikszentmihalyi has termed 'flow experiences'. These include those activities that cause you to lose track of time and induce a sense of intense delight – from listening to a favourite piece of music to completing a complicated puzzle. Flow experiences are different to the everyday activities that may only mildly distract you, one of the key differences being that they involve distinct goals and rules of performance so that you are aware of when you have accomplished them. No matter how absorbing you might find a television programme, for example, it is unlikely to induce a flow experience because it is a passive rather than an active undertaking. And passivity is not what you are aiming to increase in your life right now.

The key to eliminating loneliness and boredom in your life is not just to keep busy but to get as emotionally involved as possible in the things you do. Therefore ensure that you expand your social life with pastimes that require not just your time and energy but your spirit. This way you will increase your sense of connection with the world around you and everyone you come in contact with during these undertakings.

But let's be honest, there are times when doing things by yourself, for yourself seems less than appealing. Developing self-sufficiency and solitude takes time. In the meantime, here's a new way of finding what you need in life, that will both avoid focusing on finding a man to fill the void you may sense right now and also offer a more realistic and beneficial way of managing relationships in the future.

When we're young we usually expect someone else to satisfy our needs. This is why so many early relationships are fraught with problems – mostly because we are relatively incomplete as human beings and therefore don't know ourselves well enough to have an appreciation of what we need to feel fulfilled. Being on your own gives you the time you need to question what you want from life, and this introspection generally encourages you to realise that you cannot expect one partner to be responsible for your total happiness. The obligation for that is yours, and yours alone. Once you get in the habit of being accountable for your life, you have everything in place with which to enjoy a mature adult relationship with your significant other. And, because you have learned how to be independent, manage your life effectively and are less needy and vulnerable, you are so attractive and compelling that any man who is drawn into your life will be very special indeed.

We all need people in our lives – I don't deny that. And it is on the basis of this realisation that this next exercise has been devised. Again, find a spare sheet of paper or a blank page in your journal and begin a 'brain dump'. Write the word 'Me' in the centre of your page and draw a number of lines radiating from it, each one labelled with criteria that you have previously looked for in a partner. For example, the following nine aspects are of greatest importance to me:

- Fun and laughter
- Assisting my personal/spiritual development
- Intimacy
- Companionship
- Support with my career
- Travel companion
- Creativity catalyst
- Pragmatism
- Intellectual stimulation.

Now, alongside each of these headings, list all the people who currently contribute most to each of the areas you have specified. For example, I have certain friends with whom I have a fun time and others – quite separately – who provide me with the mental stimulation that's hugely important to me. Some people I know have made, and continue to make, a significant contribution to my career while others have helped to develop me spiritually. There are individuals in my life to whom I can always turn for help with practical tasks, while others provide a comforting shoulder to cry on, or a hug when I need it most. Include all your relevant friends, acquaintances, mentors, family members, co-workers, former lovers with whom you are still in contact, as well as people whose services you pay for (in my case, the man who mows my grass and the labourer assigned to carry out maintenance on my landlord's property).

This exercise will not only highlight just how many people there are in your life who can provide all the things you have hitherto depended on one partner to provide, but also show which areas are not well served at the moment. If there is little fun and laughter in your life right now – and let's face it, this is important to all of us – then you might want to focus on where you could meet new, amusing people. Or, if you are not getting the intellectual stimulation you crave from your current social group, then perhaps you might join a local discussion group of some sort?

You may also care to reflect on how many so-called friendships you have that don't fit into any of your listed categories. While good friendships are incredibly life-enhancing we often have a tendency to hold on to relationships, particularly with other women – including members of our own family – that have long passed their 'sell by dates'. Friendship is a two-way trade; it's about receiving as well as giving. But what if all you receive are negative experiences? If you are always having to listen to a friend constantly moan about how awful their life is, or have become the target of psychological abuse by people who constantly criticise you or say, 'You can't do that', then you must do something to remove this toxicity from your life. Good friends contribute to your personal growth. Toxic individuals stultify it. I have had occasion in the past to remove such people from my life. There was little joy in seeing them, and when I did they drained me of energy to such an extent that I had to space out our meetings just so I could re-energise myself.

A Master's thesis by Jacquelyn Mattfield of the department of psychology of Northeastern Illinois State University entitled, 'Close relationships, Meaning-in-Life and Wellbeing: A Qualitative Study of Urban Women in Late Life' (May 1996), found that friends generally fall into the following categories:

- Co-workers and playmates – people with whom you share time, interests and values.
- Help providers – reciprocal relationships involving loaning money or services.
- Confidantes – those 'shoulders to cry on' whom you can open your heart to without fear of judgement.
- Kindred spirits – those special individuals, who probably fit into all of the above categories, with whom you feel a special bond.

There is no shame in critically evaluating what you get out of your friendships. If you have difficulty thinking of anything more positive than: 'Well, we've been friends for years' then perhaps it's time to step forward into a new, more empowering life, to decide to surround yourself only with mutually supportive, loving individuals. When I was younger, to my shame, I used to just 'drop' such people from my life, never contacting them again and hoping they would simply forget about me. It's not easy to tell someone to their face that it would be best if you didn't see each other again and you must decide if and how to handle such a situation. Interestingly enough, though, you will find that as you change, all the people in your life who are unwilling or unable to raise their vibrational frequency to complement your own, will simply stop calling. If you are clear what, to you, are the essential qualities of friendship then you can benchmark all your relationships against such a list, including those men who may come into your life in the future.

My friends and I have a large number of core values in common, including a passion for life, honesty, authenticity and continuing personal growth. They are trustworthy in that I know I can say anything to them and it will not be repeated to third parties. They have put themselves out for me on those occasions when I have been desolate and have needed someone to talk to or to hug me. These are mutually beneficial relationships, although not necessarily in terms of exactly reproducing the help we provide each other with. One of my closest friends, for example, acts as a most loving and understanding surrogate mother to me, while I provide her with much-appreciated practical and financial support in return. I have developed a very high opinion of myself as a kind, loving and supportive friend and believe I deserve the same in return. Securing a strong, positive friendship base is another way in which you demonstrate that you love yourself – and there is nothing wrong in that at all.

Social activities that you choose for their own sake, because they are interesting to you, offer the sort of structure and human contact that it is important to maintain when you are living by yourself. They will redirect your thoughts to a form of positive action and encourage you to lavish on yourself the level of attention and interest that you may have heaped upon your lost partner. It is natural to feel lonely sometimes, but this state is most probably linked with missing the person you last shared your life with, not your experience of living life on your own.

Of course, there is less prospect of feeling that your life is devoid of meaning and social contact if you are able to occupy yourself with meaningful work. A fulfilling job can offer a wide variety of benefits, not least of which is financial security and independence. The right kind of work for you can foster creative and intellectual stimulation and new friendships, and can demonstrate that you can rise to, and accomplish, challenges that boost your self-confidence and self-esteem. This is why the next chapter focuses on the world of employment – but in a very specific way.

5

Discovering and Developing Your Life Purpose

'What if we are supposed to be ambitious? What if our refusal to channel our ambitions for our highest good, the highest good of those we love and the rest of the world, is the real corruption of Power?'
Sarah Ban Breathnach, *Hold That Thought: A Year's Worth of Simple Abundance*

One of the most important facets of the personal coaching and training work I offer my clients is helping them achieve a life–work balance. Together we look at a variety of different 'life areas', including relationships, work, health, money, social life, family, spiritual growth, lifelong learning and community service, and determine how much time and effort will be spent focusing on achieving a specific goal in each of them. I liken the importance of setting personal objectives and tasks in at least nine areas of life to eating a balanced diet. If we want to be physically healthy we must ensure we eat a plentiful supply of carbohydrates and protein, but also vitamins, minerals, amino acids and the various trace elements our bodies and minds require for optimal performance. Not only that, but eating only one kind of foodstuff all the time, such as bread or potatoes, is fraught with problems. For example, if there were a major shortage of the stuff then we'd either starve, or have to spend time and effort finding new foods that appeal to us and then learning how to prepare and cook them to our taste. Aside from anything else, think how boring it would be to endure the same limited menu over and over again for the rest of your life.

Similarly, if your life repertoire only consists of your relationship then when that comes to an end you suddenly find that there is nothing else in your store cupboard to sustain you: your life is suddenly a vacuum, which exacerbates a feeling of lack. You would find yourself more able to cope with the sudden disappearance of your love life if you have a thriving social life separate from that of your ex-partner, an educational or professional training programme you're committed to, or fulfilling work. Variety, as the old adage goes, is the spice of life. In the context of a balanced life it's also essential to our physical, mental, emotional and spiritual wellbeing.

However, it's true to say that not all of the life areas I discuss with my clients are equally weighted. For many people, relationships and work are the two sectors that feature most prominently. Ironically, the sexes are usually polarised when it comes to their number one priority. For many men it's their work; while for women, it's their relationships. Learning to balance both of these major areas can benefit both sexes.

Work is the principle focus of this chapter because it is so important to our sense of life purpose – a vitally important factor that we particularly need to resurrect while grieving over a relationship that has ended. But I'm not just talking about any old work. As you will shortly discover, the focus here is on your personal 'life mission'. There are particularly compelling reasons why it's important to place great emphasis on discovering and enjoying the right work for you. Loving the work you do is the best investment you can make at this time for the following reasons:

- It gives you something important to focus on, other than your ex-partner.
- Your success in this area enhances your self-esteem and self-confidence.
- Being part of an organisation or team which shares some or all of your values engenders a deeper sense of belonging.
- Going to work in whatever form – employed or self-employed, site-based or homeworking – offers you a daily structure and sense of purpose, a reason to get up in the morning.
- Earning a regular salary contributes towards your financial independence and hence self-sufficiency.
- You are more able to unleash your innate creativity.

Absorbing work – the sort in which your mind, body and spirit are totally engaged – helps you focus on something other than not having a partner, and engages you in meaningful activity while your emotional wounds are healing. After a divorce, for example, many women decide to re-enter the workplace for the first time in years in order to act on ambitions that they may have had when younger but which were subsumed by their partner's needs.

Regardless of your personal situation or reasons for working, this is a golden opportunity to put your old life behind you and present a new, reinvented 'you' to the world – one who intends to make something of her life for herself, by herself. The social aspect of work allows you to rediscover how interesting, fun, capable and friendly other people find you to be. Being in some form of employment can also help you develop platonic relationships with male co-workers that will put any animosity you may be feeling towards the opposite sex into perspective. Work is an essential component of a fulfilling life, irrespective of whether you need to earn money or not. Indeed, if you have ended up with a generous financial settlement following your divorce or other partnership split then this gives you greater flexibility in finding the work you love to do. But it's advisable not to ignore your innate longing for your life to mean something and to uniquely contribute to the world through your gifts and talents.

This is what Hesta had to say about her 'calling' as a global management consultant and now author of three books on leadership in the workplace:

I honestly believe that to do what I have to do the universe needs me to be on my own. Having been married twice before, I know there's no way I could have done what I'm doing now in that kind of relationship. I can't say whether that was just down to the people I married or whether it's my own stuff about how married women should behave. But both times I've been married the same thing happened . . . my wings were clipped.

I know I have a purpose to my life . . . I know what I have to do, and for some reason I have to be on my own to do it. The only way I can explain it is that many women have had to do the same, from Florence Nightingale to Elizabeth I. Women who have something to do out in the world. They either have a fantastic, supportive partner – something akin to a twin soul – or they are on their own. I've not yet found the former, so I'm single in order to be able to fulfil my life mission without having to justify it, ask anyone's permission or feel guilty about focusing on my work. I accept that I am meant to be on my own right now – it's part of my journey. I feel cared for, looked after and nourished by the universe, which sounds very corny but I truly believe that when I have accomplished what I am meant to I will meet someone. When I've accomplished the mission.

Hesta makes several important points here which will be explored further as you work your way through this chapter. But the one I would like to draw your attention to right now is that finding meaningful work and having a fulfilling relationship do not have to be mutually exclusive. It's just more difficult, given the way that society has been set up, to accomplish both at the same time. If your life has been geared more towards relationships and less towards finding work in which you can express your authenticity and creativity – your unique purpose for being born – then perhaps now is the time to redress this? What I am talking about with regard to work you feel passionate about should not be labelled workaholism – even if you discover you are working sixty hours a week instead of the expected forty. After all, what would benefit your life more, working for sixty hours a week at something you love and from which you gain tremendous self-confidence and self-esteem, or working for forty hours and then spending another twenty hours in front of the television?

The fascinating thing about being passionate about your work is that it is not stess-inducing. Think of it in terms of athletes committed to winning an Olympic gold medal. They can push themselves physically, mentally and emotionally towards achieving this life mission and it is not detrimental to their health. This is because having a sense of purpose and meaning lifts our spirits in a way that is hugely energising. You know deep down when your life is balanced because you feel good about yourself and your achievements. Always be aware of this and you will have nothing to worry about should others believe you are 'obsessing' about your work. The really great achievers in this life – whether in the arts, sciences, geographical exploration or business life – have needed to be totally focused in order to make their mark on life. Finding the work you love offers you the same opportunity.

Passion at work

The concept of a 'mission' can seem quite alien to most of us when referred to in terms of our work. That's because most of us have been brought up to think of work as just a job – basic employment that offers little except the ability to survive – or a career which implies movement, but says little about how much we really want to end up where we're heading. Incidentally, the word 'career' comes from the French *carriere* meaning racecourse. Which just about sums up the tendency many of us have to hurtle ever faster towards a midlife crisis in which we realise that, having climbed the ladder of success, it's been up against the wrong wall all along!

The work I'm talking about here concerns your true vocation, the most life-enhancing and innately balanced way in which you can *make a living* (an interesting term to reflect on, that), which comes from the Latin word *vocare* meaning 'to call'. And I believe that your unique calling can only be 'heard' by listening to what your heart is telling you, not just your head.

Before we look at the ways in which you can discover work that is consistent with your personal life mission and the unique contribution you are here to offer the world, let's examine some of the common ways in which women sabotage themselves in this area, starting with believing other people's perceptions of what you supposedly can or can't do.

If you had a careers adviser anything like mine your choices would have been sorely limited. In my case they focused around becoming a teacher or going to university, the implication being that this would buy me the time I needed to find what it was I wanted to do. I escaped having the other option – nursing – pushed down my throat because it was well known at school just how queasy I got at the slightest sign of blood. Actually, I knew what my calling was from an early age – it's just that no one bothered to ask about it. Ever since I could pick up a pen or found that people responded positively when I burst into song or started playacting, I wanted to be either a journalist or to work in television. Writing and communication have always been hugely important to me, yet the best suggestion my father – bless him – could come up with was for me to become a librarian. That was after he advised me to look into becoming a purser on a cruise liner because he saw how well I bossed my younger brothers about – and I loved travel.

As I discovered, when reading about multimillionaires such as the UK's Richard Branson and the US entrepreneur behind the success of the Blockbuster chain of video stores, Wayne Huizenga, the mega-successful (and wealthy) go out of their way to prove other people's opinions of them and their ideas to be wrong. This trait is shared by Erin who, in her early thirties, became a paper millionairess through the success of the beauty company she helped launch in Britain.

> Someone with no educational qualifications like me would never have gone into business if I didn't have this tendency to refuse to accept what I'm told. People never thought I was that bright as a child, and they therefore had very low expectations of me. But I never believed that I wouldn't do well. Or that I should be married, have children and live my life relying on someone else to look after me. I was determined to break the mould and I certainly did so in business. I suppose you could say it was motivating for me that I was given very limited career choices at school – I've enjoyed proving people wrong all my life.

It is common for women, particularly those of us sucked into the marriage, children and homemaker merry-go-round relatively young, to sell ourselves short. Women who are happy dedicating themselves to their families describe themselves as 'just a house-wife' while empty-nesters fear going back into the workplace because they falsely think they have no relevant skills. Yet running a home successfully isn't that different from running a business. It takes leadership, financial management, administrative and time management skills all juggled with a skill most men would find mind-boggling. *And* without a PA and wife in the background to smooth things over for us.

At a time when concepts like 'emotional intelligence' are being taken more seriously in organisations, and enhanced interpersonal skills are considered more important to service-oriented busi-nesses than traditional hard skills, women have a head start because of our innate sensitivity, intuition and nurturing abilities. In the same way that my friend Nella Barkley of the US organi-sation Life/Work Design encourages young people to re-explore their abilities and aptitudes outside school or college to see how they contribute to the new world of work, you might like to invest the time to list – in your personal journal – all the amazing skills and talents you have accrued over the years. From leading or contributing to a community group or social cause, to balancing your personal or family budget. From organising your annual vacation to preparing a weekly schedule that ensures little Johnny gets to Cubs on time while his sister Mandy never misses a dance class. From being the one person the school run mums can always rely on, to your success at battling with bureaucracy to ensure your child got into the school of your choice.

As illustrated by the millionaires mentioned earlier, life is a self-fulfilling prophecy. US self-empowerment guru Wayne Dwyer puts it this way: 'When you believe it, you'll see it.' Which, as you will have noticed, is a reversal of the way this sentence is usually expressed. If you don't have faith in yourself and your abilities then you can't expect anyone else to. And if you still don't think you have what it takes to live your mission and your dreams, then consider my story.

Having always, as I explained earlier, wanted to write or work in broadcasting, my career path had got somewhat sidetracked by the time I fell pregnant with the first of my two children. Hence I was only too happy to get out of the rat race and dedicate myself to bringing up my children – at least for the first five years of each of their lives. However, the reality was that I found being a wife and mother extremely challenging and – if I'm being honest – less than inspiring, and I needed to find something to keep myself intellectually and creatively stimulated. I started entering consumer competitions, as much for the challenge of writing clever slogans as anything else, and found that I was remarkably successful at winning prizes. After totalling something like £15,000 worth of goodies in my first year of 'comping', it occurred to me that no one had written a book on how to be successful at this rather unusual hobby. So I sat at the dining table with a basic typewriter (no home PCs in those days!) and bashed one out. It was accepted by the first publishing house I sent it to and sold a creditable number of copies.

After appearing on a local cable TV programme to promote

this book, the producer complimented me on what an extremely entertaining guest I had been. Sensing a wonderful opportunity to get on the 'box' on a regular basis, I asked her if she'd be interested in my researching and presenting short outside broadcasts in which I talked to local people about their unusual hobbies. She said yes, and from those humble beginnings my broadcasting and subsequent journalistic career was born. I worked without being paid for a magazine, while I amassed a whole range of cuttings that I could then send out to other publications. Never being a great one for starting at the bottom, I contacted a national daily newspaper while I was acting as roving reporter for a pan-European satellite channel and asked if they needed any help with articles. There was a freelance research position they were looking for someone to fill. I jumped at it and, before long, was writing my own articles. That led to my writing books, which led to setting up my own business as a motivational speaker and personal development workshop designer and facilitator – all the time not having a single, relevant professional qualification.

And do you know the interesting thing? No one asked me or seemed to care. Even when, years after establishing a very successful freelance journalism career for myself, I achieved my diploma in journalism, this made absolutely no difference to the amount of work I got or the money I was paid. I have been offered editorships, TV programmes, regular guest slots on radio, and corporate training work largely on the basis of my ongoing reputation as someone who delivers what she promises. And that reputation was built on my belief that I could do anything I set my mind to.

That's the point about a 'calling' – you have to listen and then act in order to make it a reality. I believe life constantly presents us with opportunities that are largely missed because of false beliefs, which have usually come about because of what other people have told us about what we can or can't achieve. The stories we tell ourselves are incredibly powerful, yet often quite debilitating, because we're focused on what we can't do and not what we can. And yet, you can opt to rewrite your personal narrative any time you like. If you are committed to finding the work you were born to do which, as Kahlil Gibran expressed it in his magnificent work *The Prophet*, fulfils 'a part of earth's fondest dream assigned to you when that dream is born', then I urge you to outline your personal history in your journal starting from the messages you received from your parents and teachers to how you have experienced life subsequently.

Examine the assumptions, beliefs, attitudes, habits and behaviour patterns – positive and negative – which have directly, or indirectly, influenced everything that has happened to you in your life so far. Then, by yourself or with the help of a trusted friend or professional coach, highlight those habits which do not serve you well and determine to focus on the more empowering ones.

There are many inspiring examples of people who have achieved all sorts of amazing things through the power of self-belief (and, remember, the more you tell yourself something the more you will believe it, even if in the beginning you don't!), including the former world heavyweight boxing champion, Mohammed Ali. As you may remember, his catch phrase was 'I am the greatest.' The interesting thing is that Ali was telling this to everyone who would listen, even before he was a boxing champion and was fighting under the name of Cassius Clay. This inspirational man knew intuitively that others would only believe in his abilities if he believed in himself. And the most immediate way you can demonstrate self-belief is through telling people how wonderful you are.

Can you imagine yourself going around saying, 'I am the greatest'? If not, then maybe this was because your parents or carers felt they had to knock the 'arrogance' and 'big-headedness' out of you when you were a child, in order to make sure you fitted in with the rest of a largely average society. Ponder instead on the advice of US spiritual author Marianne Williamson who, in her book *A Return to Love*, urges each one of us to remember that, 'Your playing small doesn't serve the world ... We are all meant to shine.'

Before you say that there are too many difficulties in your life for you to ever live your dreams, think of the women throughout history who have been challenged in some way or other in order to express themselves authentically. The glittering prizes never come easy – some trade-off is always required, and one of these may be working towards your mission without a partner, either temporarily or (more rarely) permanently. While Hesta mentioned the more well known examples of Florence Nightingale and Queen Elizabeth I of England as women who eschewed partnership in order to dedicate themselves to their destinies, there are countless others who serve as similarly inspiring role models, such as the novelists Jane Austen, Emily Brontë and Anna Sewell, author of *Black Beauty*. Or social reformers like Dame Lilian Barker, Dorothea Beale and Dorothy Pelo, the latter being the first woman in Britain to command and train a force of women when she became Superintendent of the Metropolitan Women's Police. There have been pioneering scientists such as Mary Anning, the geologist who discovered many previously unknown dinosaur remains, Elizabeth Blackwell, the UK's first woman physician, and Rosalind Franklin, whose important contribution to the structure of DNA has not been widely recognised.

I urge you to read about the likes of the nineteenth- and twentieth-century feminist barrister Chrystal Macmillan, who worked tirelessly towards improving women's status and wages in industry and in the general area of equality of citizenship. Or impresarios Annie Horniman, Italia Conti and Lilian Baylis, all of whom dedicated their lives to the theatre – the latter being the founder of the Old Vic and Sadler's Wells companies, and who believed she was divinely inspired to accomplish her work.

All these amazing women lived during times when females could not automatically expect the same educational and social opportunities as males. Yet all of them, despite the odds, helped shape history and strongly influenced the course of world events. I don't believe it is a coincidence that in order to do this, all chose to remain single.

Could it be that your focus on relationships has distracted you from answering your calling? By exploring this possibility in the rest of this chapter, two things could happen. First, you discover that your work offers you greater fulfilment and a sense of achievement than your relationships ever have. Second, that by focusing on something other than finding a man to share your life with, you become so empowered, whole and compelling that the one man who is your intellectual, emotional and spiritual equal is magnetically drawn to you.

Defining passionate work

As you will have gathered by now, the sort of occupation we are talking about here isn't the usual humdrum, task-oriented employment commonly associated with the word 'work'. In the following exercises you will be encouraged to explore the work that speaks to your heart, that keeps you intellectually and creatively stimulated, and demonstrates who you are as a person, not merely the skills and qualifications you have accrued.

In order to recognise your 'calling', it is important to think about activities, situations and environments in which you have had the following experiences:

- Time loses its meaning – either by speeding up or slowing down, associated with 'flow experiences' (see page 103)
- Your actual performance is way beyond your normal capabilities – you find you challenge your usual limitations physically, mentally and emotionally
- Your energy levels are unusually high during and afterwards
- They are preceded by a sense of excitement and anticipation
- You dream about them
- You are consistently enthusiastic about them
- You feel confident and empowered while undertaking them
- Others notice and express their admiration of you
- You are given support and assistance easily – you feel 'lucky'
- You feel 'complete'.

Bearing in mind all the above, now answer the following two questions:

1. If you could devise for yourself the perfect job, what would it be like?
2. What are you most passionate about?

Your replies hold the key to unlocking whatever it is within you that demonstrates your vocation in life – whether that be in business, education, the arts, community projects, political initiatives or social causes nearer to home. First find out what fires you up by identifying past examples of the points listed above, and then look for a pattern in terms of the kind of activities, environments and people that help fuel your passion.

Next, look for ways in which that might be translated into business behaviour. We all have preferred thinking styles or mental aptitudes that are highly suggestive of the sort of work which turns us on. For example, I thrive on the right brain processes of feelings, intuition and the imagination. I'm a 'big picture', conceptual person who is fairly comfortable – though not passionately so – dealing with details, and needs plenty of variety and change. I enjoy being with people, but not all the time, and can work extremely effectively for periods in which I have no physical contact whatsoever. Therefore writing books and articles plus devising workshops with occasional forays into motivational speaking and facilitation are perfect forms of expression for me. Not only are these activities that I do best, but I experience a sense of meaning and purpose from undertaking them. Whereas working in an office, adhering to organisational rules, doing regular, highly procedural work involving quantifiables according to someone else's deadline, as I did before I had my children, is anathema to me.

Ironically, by understanding my preferred thinking styles I also engage my heart. So now let's see in which of the following four categories your strengths and passions might lie:

Left brain dominant
The analytical self
Loves logical problem solving, scientific methodology, statistics, diagnostics, abstract, fact-based work – i.e. areas in which logical thought is an asset.

The perceptual self
Is linked to organising, administration, formulating policies, supervisory work, legal or mechanical activities, setting up and controlling operations – i.e. anything that benefits from planning, detail and procedures.

Right brain dominant
The creative self
Has a tendency to be attracted to entrepreneurial activities, intuitive problem solving, strategising, visualising, designing, innovating, leadership, selling, various artistic endeavours and communicating in a large-scale way.

The interpersonal self
Encompasses facilitating, teaching, co-ordinating, service to others, nurturing, caring, counselling, healing, supporting and any emotional, kinaesthetic-based activities.

Clearly, the majority of us straddle more than one of these brain dominance quadrants and that widens the range of work which appeals to us, at least theoretically. The important thing to remember when looking to discover and develop your life purpose, is to consider which type of work on your list speaks to your heart as well as your head. Then, *and only then*, should you start to appraise the skills, qualifications and experience you will need to accomplish your dream. Don't forget that in today's service-oriented world of work, highly self-motivated, passionate, 'can do' individuals have a magnetism that is considerably more valu-able to employers than those who look good on paper but cause customers to turn off in droves, never to return, because they don't love what they do. As my experience illustrates – and that of countless other women who have built their working lives on a driving passion and strong self-belief – the key to finding the work you love is to:

- First, believe it is possible.
- Then, build up a picture of what kind of work this might be. Realise that your past experiences both inside and outside the workplace contain many of the clues you need to piece together the kind of work you would feel passionate about. It is particularly valuable to realise what did *not* suit you as much as what did.
- Consider not just the 'what' (the kind of work that interests you, based on your thinking preferences or mental motivations), but also the 'who' (the kind of people you work best for and alongside), the 'where' (the nature of your working environment – office or 'on the road', open plan or sectionalised, a place where you have constant contact with people, or work pretty much by yourself), the 'when' (full time or part time, according to specific projects with periods of time off for travel, training and development etc., or strictly nine-to-five, forty-eight weeks a year), and, finally, the 'how' (staff or freelance, employed or self-employed).
- Draw up a shopping list itemising all the characteristics of the ideal work you desire, to use as a check-list when you receive interviews and job offers.
- Compile a complete list of all the skills – 'soft' (personal and interpersonal) and 'hard' (specific job-related qualifications, abilities and experience) – that you have accrued over the years, irrespective of whether you have done so in a paid, traditional working environment or not. Don't leave anything out, and when you think you have completed this, ask a close friend or family member to look at it to see what could be added.
- Network – officially and unofficially. Tell as many people as possible about the kind of work you are looking for, as much to find out whether you need to add to your portfolio of skills as

anything else. Investigate the kinds of positions relevant employers, those who can offer work you feel passionate about, are looking to fill. But don't get too caught up believing you have to be fully qualified or experienced before dipping your toes into the work pool. Many people, including myself, have landed themselves dream positions just by being in the right place at the right time, because the clearer you are about your passions and life purpose, the more the universe has a tendency to support you. Looked at from a less spiritual perspective, you could simply say that – in the same way as when you are planning to buy a specific model of car you spot rather a lot of them out on the road – just bringing something into consciousness reinforces your ability to spot opportunities when they arise.

- However, if you passionately want to work in an area for which there is an obvious gap in your skills, qualifications or experience, do what you can to plug it as soon as possible.

- Don't discount temping (where relevant) as a way of getting a foot into a specific line of work or organisation. Not only can this be a very lucrative and flexible form of employment but it also puts you in direct contact with people and information that could lead to full-time employment.

- Finally, take the initiative, be cheeky, sell yourself enthusiastically, give more than is expected, and live your dream even before it has come to fruition. There are very few human beings, regardless of what exalted positions they hold, who don't at some time or other think to themselves, 'I'm surely going to get found out!', because we don't think we're worthy to hold down really fulfilling, exciting jobs. Yet the truth is, our jobs are rarely as big as our soul's potential and that latency will not be confined by your gender, educational background, professional skills or experience. An inspiring example of this is the film *Erin Brockovich*, starring Julia Roberts. As a single mother on the breadline she foists herself on the law firm who failed to win her lawsuit against a driver who crashed into her car, causing whiplash. Based on a true story, the heroine's only talents at the beginning of the film appear to be a scant regard for authority, a vicious temper and a degree of persistence that would put a pit bull terrier to shame. Yet the woman's passion for achieving justice for the victims of corporate negligence causes her to run rings around the top legal experts and law graduates she comes into contact with.

Once you have found the work which speaks to your heart and soul, it's tempting to think that because you have a regular income you'll have no money worries. The sad fact is that women generally leave financial matters to their male partners and therefore have little or no experience in managing money. Yet there is no reason why you can't be as adept in this area of your life as in any other – and that's what the next chapter is all about. Although you may not believe it now, it's not the lack of money that causes you to get into debt – as countless divorcees have claimed to me in the past – but inappropriate spending. In short, spending more than you earn. If you are finding yourself constantly short of cash because your husband has walked out or divorced you, or your partner has died without leaving you with adequate provision, please don't believe that this is a principal cause of your unhappiness. Having all the money in the world won't make you happier or more contented, nor will it make you feel more financially secure. As Dr Joy Brown states in her book *The Nine Fantasies That Will Ruin Your Life*: 'If money were the key to happiness, millionaires wouldn't have ulcers. They do, and it's not.'

Plus, think of the high earners in the entertainment industry – actors like Burt Reynolds and Debbie Reynolds, rap star M. C. Hammer, and film director Francis Ford Coppola - who have filed for bankruptcy and continue to do so. The richest nation on earth, the United States of America, files the highest number of bankruptcies every year – more than one million of them. The fact that, in the US, savings represent just 4.8 per cent of the average income, and consumer debt hit a record $1.25 trillion in 1997 is not unrelated to this extremely stressful – yet usually unnecessary – state of affairs.

In the next chapter, I want to help you take charge of your financial affairs, regardless of how much or how little you earn, so that money helps enhance your single lifestyle, and does not detract from it. More than anything else I want to convince you that, even if you've never balanced a chequebook in your life or believe you have no head for money, you don't need a man in your life – or his money - in order to live the life you deserve. On the contrary, successfully managing your own money is another way in which you can boost your self-confidence and self-esteem while creating a wonderful, single life.

6

Taking Charge

'MYTH NO 2: My husband (or some other man) will take care of me.'

David Bach, *Smart Women Finish Rich*

I'd like you to forget for a moment that this chapter focuses on your financial situation and how to improve it so that you never again doubt your ability to handle money effectively. Before we engage in any discussion as to how or why it's important for you to take charge of your fiscal affairs, I want you to undertake an exercise that I ask all my clients to complete before I begin their life coaching programme. Believe me, this is such a powerful activity that it will transform the way you think about and maintain your money, giving you the financial freedom to live life exactly as you choose; so it's worth taking the time to do it properly. All you need to devote to it is thirty minutes to one hour. That's not much of a sacrifice to make, wouldn't you agree, to change your financial future for the better?

You may want to make your notes on a separate sheet of paper or write them directly in your journal. The only other thing I ask you to do is to find somewhere quiet where you can relax and concentrate without interruption. When you've done this, consider this question: What are the most important things in the world to you?

Don't panic if your mind seems to have gone blank. Just take a few deep breaths and let that question float around in your mind for a while. Think of it another way: If your life goal – as it is for the vast majority of human beings – is to be happy, what would you need to have to fulfil that desire for inner contentment?

How we define happiness, and what it means to each of us, is very different, so you may need to think about this for a while. Is it security that is of paramount importance to you? Or your independence? Constantly having some sort of intellectual challenge? Finding your soulmate? (Yes, that's quite okay – remember, this isn't a book against relationships, only one that promotes having the best possible relationship with yourself.) Here are some of the most common themes that crop up when I ask people what happiness means to them. This list is by no means exhaustive, and rather than be unduly influenced by these words, it's important that you come up with your own definition of fulfilment:

Variety	High financial reward	Creative expression
Good health	Power and influence	Reputation
Freedom	Intellectual challenge	Living with passion
Strong family bond	Public recognition/status	Sense of belonging
Full social life	Making a difference	Independence
Self-respect	Appreciation	Loving life partner
Balance	Being altruistic	Inner satisfaction
Spiritual enlightenment	Security	Being 'the best'

Once you have considered the above questions carefully, you should be in a position to understand more clearly what in life is most important to you – the 'drivers' that make life meaningful and fulfilled from your personal perspective. It's unlikely that you will want to confine yourself to just two or three of these, so write down all the things which intuitively appear the most compelling and represent – to you – the achievement of a totally blissful life.

When you have done this I'd like to offer you my

congratulations. Because you have just identified your core values or guiding principles. These are the foundation upon which you will most successfully build anything of importance in your life – whether it be your career, your relationship with a partner or a thriving social life. In fact, it would be true to say that without knowing your values none of your life goals is likely to be accomplished. That's why business organisations have mission statements outlining their purpose which, in the most enlightened of cases, say nothing about making money or about the products or services they offer and everything about deeper reasons for their existence. In the case of one pharmaceutical company it is 'to alleviate pain and disease'; another articulates it as 'making a positive contribution to people's lives'; yet another, 'being in the business of preserving and improving human life'. In all of these cases the focus is on the *why* and not the *what*. When you know why things are important to you, you have a sense of meaning. And it is this sense of worth that not only powerfully moves you forward in your life but also so elegantly impacts on the lives of others too.

You might still be wondering what this has got to do with managing your money. Bear with me for a moment – we'll be coming to that shortly. There's just a little more of this exercise still to complete. You should by now have a list of values in front of you. I'd like you to sort them into a hierarchy with your most important value at the top, decreasing in importance as you work your way down the list. You may want to limit yourself to five values. In any event, I suggest you work with no more than ten. You can construct your hierarchy in several ways. I suggest the following, although follow your own method if you'd prefer:

- Write or type all your chosen values on to a sheet of paper, allowing plenty of space between the words. Cut around each word so you end up with a maximum of ten small pieces of paper, each of which contains one value.
- Look quickly through your list and intuitively position the words in an order that you think is most representative of your

personal desires – the highly preferred ones at the top, and the less preferred ones at the bottom.

- Taking one word at a time, score it mentally against each of the other words, asking yourself which is the most important. For example, is 'Making a difference' more important than 'High financial reward' and 'High financial reward' more important than 'A full social life' etc.? In this way you can check whether your intuitive response was accurate.

Whatever you do, please be honest with yourself. There are no right or wrong answers, and if you try to fool yourself that something is important to you when it is not, then the foundation upon which you're going to build your new, more empowered approach to life will be shaky. This exercise is totally private and is about what gives meaning to your life, not what others think you 'must', 'should' or 'ought' to believe. Remember, life is full of trade-offs and it is important to be aware of this in order to maintain your integrity. This is why you're being asked to spend so much time on this list. Think of it as piecing together a jigsaw puzzle from which you will glean a picture of your inner self, the unique homing signal that will undeniably lead you towards the life you long – and deserve – to have.

With your hierarchy of values in front of you, ask yourself whether these are reflected in the way you manage your finances? For example, one 42-year-old client called Martha told me that her top five life values were:

1. Security
2. Independence
3. Freedom
4. Self-respect
5. Creative expression.

Yet when we looked at her financial situation none of these values were apparent. She had no pension plan or health insurance and had not made a will – so how 'secure' was that likely to make her feel as she got older? Martha regularly spent so much every month on her credit cards that she reneged on an earlier promise to herself to pay off the balance each month in order to avoid high interest charges. This meant that she needed to shackle herself to a high-paying job (Note: there is no reference to 'High financial reward' in the above list!) in order to meet her increasing financial obligations. Is that kind of action consistent with putting a high priority on independence, freedom, self-respect and the desire for creative expression? No wonder Martha's life was a treadmill of unhappiness – she was living a life completely out of sync with what, deep down, was important to her.

Once Martha recognised the need to underpin every decision and action with her life values, she began to transform her financial situation. She came to terms with the key factor that separates the rich from the not-so-rich: Martha stopped filling her life with liabilities and started to build up her assets. Instead of frittering away her hard-earned money on things that only gave her temporary pleasure (and sometimes not even that, given the stress she put herself under every time a credit card bill plopped on to her doormat), she took a long, hard look at her spending habits. She recognised the emotional drain of driving a top-of-the-range convertible that had lost half its value in under eighteen months, or the five-star hotel lifestyle she'd got into the habit of. Martha had once joked that she preferred to invest in her psychological wellbeing by trawling the New York stores four times a year rather than put money into a health plan, but her laughter rang hollow. In truth, she was deeply concerned about the future as a single woman, with no partner's income or pension contributions to fall back on.

Females have traditionally short-changed themselves by believing that men are better at managing money. They are not. Tell that to the women who've found their lifestyles threatened by their partner's gambling, poor investment decisions or other dysfunctional habits. Nor is developing good financial skills only important while you are single. With the increasing tendency of couples not to marry, or to separate after just a few years together, it's becoming more and more the norm for individuals to keep their financial affairs separate from those of their partners. This is because people are realising that sharing works both ways, and you can get stuck with your lover's liabilities as well as their assets. Joint accounts were all very well in the days when couples were taxed according to the fact that men were the main breadwinners in the family. But in the UK, women have enjoyed tax independence for almost a decade, even if the rest of their financial affairs don't reflect that autonomy.

Psychologically, too, it's vitally important for your self-esteem to have money which is yours. I'm sure many women have experienced something similar to my mother, who suffered the indignity of having to ask for every penny she spent, and who was denied many treats because my father didn't deem it important enough for him to put his hands in his pockets – even though she had cooked, cleaned and cared for him for decades and had borne him five children.

If you get into good money habits now, then if you choose to share your life with a partner in the future, you will be doing so from a basis of equality, not the disparity that the majority of women have had to put up with for so long. After all, once you are a woman who is competent with money and handles her finances astutely, you'll be more inclined to want – and hence find – a partner with similar values. Which bodes very well for the strength and length of any future relationship, as it has been found that a positive financial situation – only possible through good money management skills – is a contributory factor to couples staying together. Indeed, a study by the UK's Department of Social Security found that the risk of marital and relationship break-ups is reduced by almost a third when couples are flush with cash. And according to the UK counselling service Relate, conflicts over money contribute most to domestic arguments.

There has never been a better time to find basic advice about money management. The Internet is an excellent place to start. You will find countless professional sites devoted to women's money matters, catering for everyone from those deep in debt to sophisticated stock market investors. Unfortunately for those living outside North America, the majority of these sites are geared to the US market, but a lot of the information is still generally relevant and new material is being posted all the time. Try searching for topics like 'women and money', 'female money management' and 'financial advice for women'. Apart from advice on managing your money, you'll be able to:

- Get access to free general, expert advice on everything from cutting childcare costs and pre-divorce strategies to establishing an investment portfolio.
- Post a query about your financial situation and get a personalised reply.
- Use interactive tools that will show you how to reduce your debt, estimate your tax or plan for your retirement.
- Benefit from sharing the experience of other women through support group and chat rooms devoted to money matters.
- Search for the latest books on financial strategies for women.
- Find relevant articles from magazines like the US publication *Money for Women* (www.money.com).
- Discover how to find or start a women's investment club in your area that will help you learn about, and earn from, stocks and shares.

It is outside the scope of this book to go into the subject of more effectively managing your money in any great depth, which is why accessing websites, books and money magazines is important. However, I would like to offer you the following suggestions. Not only are they geared towards encouraging you to face your financial reality but will, if adhered to consistently, reap untold rewards.

Effect a money makeover and take the mystery out of financial mastery

Attitude

As we discovered in Chapter Three, your attitude to something has a direct bearing on your subsequent experience of it. And so it is with money. Unfortunately, many women have burdened themselves with the belief that they are no good at financial matters. Yet the facts indicate otherwise: in the United States where investment clubs are thriving, almost 70 per cent of the members of the National Association of Investors Corporation (NAIC) are women, an increase of 30 per cent in the last decade. More importantly, the women-only clubs are out-performing their male equivalents, and have done so in nine out of the last twelve years.

Women have the advantage of bringing their hearts as well as their heads into any equation which, combined with our organisational skills and the fact that we're comfortable asking for more information about things we don't know about, can give us the edge in money matters. If only we could learn to applaud and not decry these innate abilities.

Don't let the habit of handing over responsibility for financial dealings to the men in your life – be they your father, partner or employer – blind you to the fact that you can manage money when you put your mind to it. There must be at least one occasion in the past when you took charge of your finances and it paid off. I urge you to dive into your memory to find it.

If your belief about your ability to handle financial matters changes for the worst when there's a man around, then you have to ask yourself why. This is a common tendency, as Jemma's story about her mother illustrates:

My father was a very dynamic businessman when he met and married my mother in the 1940s. As a child, I always remembered her as totally submissive, never contradicting him or going against his wishes. I never thought of her as being anything other than a timid woman with a very high inferiority complex. Yet when father died she successfully took over the running of the family's lumber construction company, with no business experience whatsoever. She had trained as a nurse when younger but stopped working as soon as she was married because that's what Daddy wanted. Mom was widowed at forty-seven and told me later that the business gave her a reason to get up in the morning.

Then she met my stepfather, whom she'd known in High School. He, also, was a business executive and I watched her fall back into the trap of being the subservient wife. Within a few years of her remarriage she had sold the company to my stepbrother and, with it, all her sense of independence. I can't understand it. For me the high self-esteem and confidence that comes from running my own business – from the financial side to marketing – is a powerful drug. Why would Mom want to give that up? It just seems that for women like my mother, and the girlfriends who've dumped me as soon as they find a man, they become so focused on his life that they're prepared to lose their own.

I repeat – think back to a time when you have successfully handled money before, even if it was way back when you saved enough of your pocket money to buy a bike or pay for a holiday without your parents' help. Whatever you've done once you can do again. Believe it.

Bad habits

We all have them. But you're only going to deal with them effectively, once and for all, when you bring these negatives out into the open. Here are some of the things I've done in the past (and, if I'm being honest, still succumb to from time to time):

- Withdrawing too much cash at one time and then frittering it away without keeping track of where it's gone.
- Using my credit cards to pay for impulse buys that I'd think

twice about if I were paying by cash.
- Failing to regularly put away, in a separate savings account, money to pay the VAT and tax man.
- Not saving any of my income and living life to the hilt.
- Not accurately knowing what my monthly expenses are.
- Failing to keep a note of cashpoint withdrawals.
- Splashing out on clothes I don't need or an expensive meal (with champagne!) to cheer myself up – usually about money problems.
- Believing, like Mr Micawber, that something will always turn up, thereby having no pension plan or health insurance.
- Failing to keep track of my bank statement with the optimistic belief that the bank always gets things right (they don't!).
- Preferring to ignore my parlous financial situation rather than taking practical steps to improve it.

Admittedly, many of these bad habits were ones I indulged in during my marriage. Unfortunately, once I was divorced, lost access to my husband's high five-figure salary and had to live on my own meagre income, I tried to ignore the fact that my circumstances had changed by maintaining the same behaviour. Until, so stressed out from worrying about how I was going to clear my credit card debt and pay my tax bill on time, I finally shocked myself into getting to grips with my situation.

I'd like you to write down all the bad habits that you've got with regards to money, on a sheet of paper or in your journal. Then consider what has caused them. Perhaps, like I was, you are angry at your ex-partner and consider him responsible for your never having any money. How does spending more than you have help you in the long run? Who is hurt more by your failure to control your finances? Believe me, being successful and happy are the best ways of getting revenge for the financial withholding that many men are guilty of after a relationship split. Most importantly, don't allow money mismanagement to erode your self-esteem at a time when it is the foundation upon which your new life is to be built.

Cutting back

Ask any expert on effective money management and they will tell you the same thing: It's not what you earn that determines whether you'll be rich or poor. It's how much you spend.

Consider these two examples:

Connie earns £75,000 a year, is mortgaged to the hilt, drips with gold jewellery and changes her top-of-the-range sports car every three to four years. Her annual expenditure tops £100,000, and she engages in a constant juggling act with store cards and credit facilities to cope with the deficit. She maintains that, because she is such a high earner, she can sort herself out financially whenever she chooses. It's just that she's never got round to it and therefore has no savings, no pension plan and no health insurance. Nothing Connie wears, drives or does is either owned outright by her or has come without some hidden extra cost due to the interest she pays on her credit cards and loans.

Meg, on the other hand, earns £20,000 a year. She lives modestly in a house with a mortgage much smaller than the equity she owns in it, which she plans to use towards securing early retirement. Meg keeps check of everything she spends and forces herself to wait for at least twenty-four hours before making a decision to buy anything over £250. Most of the time she decides the item is not necessary to her life after all. Meg saves a portion of her salary every month, some of it in a retirement plan, some in a savings account where the high interest rate helps pay for her annual vacation to an exotic location.

Compared with Connie, Meg is the richer, even though she earns less than a third of the other woman's salary. And Meg's future financial situation is certainly more secure. Read any book about how self-made millionaires accumulated their fortune and you'll discover that they live extremely frugally in comparison to their wealth. In contrast there are those whom someone once described to me as 'fur coat and no knickers people': individuals who have the external trappings of wealth but who, like Connie, don't own anything outright, and whose financial stability is precarious in the extreme because they spend far more than they earn.

Do you know, to the penny, how much your monthly expenses are and the extent to which they fluctuate through the year? One simple exercise that paved the way for me to take a more realistic approach to managing my money is this: keep a small notebook with you and jot down every penny you spend each day, and on what. Do this for at least a month. Make a note of everything – no matter how minor, including the coffee and doughnut you buy on the way to work, the newspapers you read every day, your bus fares, even the coin you popped into the charity collector's box. Then, at the end of one month, add up what your expenses have been and review that against your income. You'll probably be horrified to find the amount of money that haemorrhages out of your bank account on things that add little or no value to your life.

It's up to you to decide whether you want to be comfortably off by taking control of your expenses NOW and saving at least 10 per cent of your income every month – or continue living from hand to mouth. Not too excited by the thought of cutting back, huh? Well, here are a few facts that motivated me to get to grips with my dysfunctional spending habits and hopefully will do the same for you.

I had never considered how, the longer I put off saving, the more it was going to cost me to achieve security – one of my principle values in life. Not until I came across a book I can highly recommend entitled *Smart Women Finish Rich*, written by US money coach David Bach. In it the author outlined how, had I started saving a decade ago, I would only need to put aside a couple of thousand pounds a year earning good interest in order to accrue £660,000 by the time I'm sixty-five. Today, the amount I need to save to accomplish that level of security is way outside my current earning abilities so I will have to settle for less of a financial safeguard when I am older. More importantly, for every year I delay that decision to save, my retirement package will be smaller and smaller until it reaches the point where I may have to work until I lose the use of my hands or eyesight or both in order to maintain my current standard of living. That worries the hell out of me!

You may not want or need such a high sum at retirement. But the fact remains – as a single woman you have only your own finances to fall back on. Like me, you don't have the luxury of a second income. Look at your list of values from the earlier exercise and honestly review what approach best demonstrates those guiding principles. What would benefit you the most – saving a little on a regular basis, or spending way beyond your means? In any event, are the things you are buying today really contributing to your life in any meaningful way?

Design a money plan

Only a small part of the work I do coaching clients to live more fulfilled and balanced lives involves identifying their core values (see p. 128) and helping them sets goals in line with those guiding principles. Unfortunately, life does not conform to what we say we want or even to what we visualise. To make things happen in our lives we need to take action, and what underpins all effective action is planning, the sort of detailed planning you would automatically do if you were arranging a vacation or moving house.

The chart on pp. 145 to 147 will help you clarify the action you need to take to get your financial affairs in order. Before you start to fill it in, I'd like you to engage in another visualisation exercise. This one can be applied to any, or all, areas of your life, although we are going to focus solely on your financial future for now. Before we start, let me relate a fascinating story about the power of creative imagery. While I'm not saying that visualising will magically transform your life exactly as you envisage it (as happened in the following story), it is a potent, ineffable force that can make a huge difference to your future reality.

As is common in the entertainment industry, the career of US movie star Jim Carrey (*Batman Forever*, *Man on the Moon*) wasn't always as glittering as it is today. Indeed, in the late 1980s, even the occasional TV work he was being offered seemed to be drying up. One evening, he drove himself up into the Hollywood Hills and began to daydream about what life would be like when he was rich and famous. With that in mind, Carrey got out his cheque book and wrote himself a cheque for $10 million, dating it Thanksgiving Day 1995. Every time he felt his dream of stardom was slipping away, he would take out that cheque and recreate the positive mental and physical sensations he had felt during that earlier visualisation experience. As it happened, life did take a miraculous turn for Jim Carrey, his talent was spotted, and he was offered lead roles in films like *Ace Ventura, Pet Detective* and *The Mask*. In November 1995 he was offered $10 million to star in the *The Mask 2* – the amount, month and year that appeared on the cheque he had carried around for all those years in his wallet.

Visualisation exercise

Make sure you are in a place in which you feel relaxed and comfortable, where you will not be disturbed. Imagine a time, not too far in the future, when you will be living life according to the values you identified in your personal hierarchy. Focusing specifically on your financial status, in your mind's eye work your way through the following questions, always visualising your *future*:

- What kind of life is it?
- How does it make you feel?
- Why do you feel that way?
- How different is your life now to how it was before you decided to make certain changes to it?
- What sort of people are in your life?
- Who are your friends and are they different from the people that you used to know?
- What is your living environment like?
- Where do you live? Describe this in as much detail as possible
- What do your daily activities comprise?

- What sort of work are you, or have you been, doing that has contributed to this ideal life?

If at any time you feel less than 100 per cent enthralled, excited and fulfilled in your future life with regard to your financial security ask yourself – what is missing? What needs to be included so that your life is as financially satisfying and complete as it can be?

Your future reality

Once you have imagined a future in which all your personal needs and desires are met you are then in a better position to make it a reality. Buy a journal or a pad of paper and write down, in as much detail as you can, the financial future that you have imagined for yourself. If necessary go back into a state of visualisation and, using all your senses of taste, touch, smell, vision, hearing and intuition, outline everything that has made a contribution towards this ideal life. Then ask yourself the following questions:

1. What are the most significant differences between my life now and how I intend it to be in the future?
2. Taking each of those differences one at a time – the tension between what you are/have and what you will be/have – what incremental changes can you begin to make that will lead you to that ideal future? Thinking about the guiding principles outlined in your personal hierarchy, how many of them currently influence the way you manage your money? What changes do you need to make to ensure they influence your day-to-day money management more fully?
3. What time-frame are you going to put on this future life? Will this be you in five, ten, fifteen or twenty years' time? Be specific as to when you want this ideal to become a reality.

The above exercise will supply you with the information you will need to draw up a timetable for yourself, breaking down each of your goals into objectives, plans and tasks that you can accomplish one day at a time, but which will inevitably lead you towards the future that you have just visualised.

Here are some suggestions to help you complete the chart on pp. 145 to 147:

Vision Statement

Using your personal hierarchy of values as a guideline, create a statement describing in 'big picture' terms what is important to you – the principles by which you intend to manage your money.

Example: 'I commit to the sort of financial practices and money management that offer me a secure future in which I can retire comfortably and have no worries about meeting health bills, which will provide me with the freedom to take on jobs/projects that fulfil my desire for passion, freedom and variety in my work.'

Goals

These represent the intentions you need to focus on to move you into your envisioned future life. Ensure these are stated in the positive – it's about what you want from life, not what you want to get rid of/change. I suggest, rather than overwhelming yourself, that you identify just three goals to focus on for now – perhaps linked to a short, medium and long-term period.

Example:

Goal 1: Investigate and commence a pension plan that will allow me to retire at age fifty-six, providing £25,000 p.a.

Goal 2: Check out the most appropriate health insurance for my needs and commit to this.

Goal 3: Have saved the equivalent of six months' living expenses within two years.

Time-frame/deadlines

Be sure to specify by what date you will commit to achieving each of your goals and tasks. Will that be in days, months or even years from now? Setting time-frames is not always as easy as it might seem. Try to avoid making these unrealistically short. Attempting to secure a major goal like reducing all credit card debts in a few months might be highly appealing, but just how practical is that? Always steer a middle course between motivatory short deadlines that, if missed, end up being counter-productive and goals that are so far in the future that they fail to inspire you to take action now.

Potential challenges and ways to overcome them

Any endeavour in which you want to be successful requires you to reflect on the challenges that you will face. After all, it's only human to slip into bad habits now and again, no matter how much you want to change. Ask yourself what might stop you achieving the goals you have set for yourself. Again, be honest and realistic. If you identify that your credit card spending gets out of control when you feel low or depressed, don't just commit to cutting up your cards or handing them over temporarily to someone you trust. Look for the causes of your negative moods and do what you can to eliminate or mitigate them. Don't get caught up blaming or involving other people for potential problems, focus only on those things over which you have control. Think about external situations, e.g. 'I believe I deserve a higher salary for the job I'm doing and will therefore either ask for a raise or find another position', and internal situations, e.g. developmental blocks that you may need to overcome, e.g. 'I find it difficult to motivate myself, therefore I need to find a close friend or professional coach who will keep me on track with my commitment to save 10 per cent of my income each month'. Then set realistic deadlines by which to achieve these commitments.

Tasks

Tasks are the smaller, incremental steps you need to undertake to achieve your goals. Look at the challenges you have identified that may be preventing you from realising your goals and ensure some of 'to do's include plans for eliminating these external hurdles or internal developmental blocks.

For example, if you recognise that you need help to keep yourself motivated to save, you might choose to investigate the nature and cost of a personal coach who specialises in this particular life area.

Personal strengths

This is a particularly important section to complete in your chart because it will demonstrate that you do indeed have the resources you need to turn your life around. Please don't be modest here. It's one thing to be honest and realistic about your weaknesses, but it's vital to balance this by identifying the qualities that are innate or which you have developed that will help move you from where you are to where you want to be.

Achievements

List here all the things you are proud of that relate to the financial sector of your life. For example: 'I've bought my own place and have a large equity in that property'; 'I pay off my credit card bills every month without fail'; 'I have no debts'; 'I can afford to go on two foreign holidays each year.' Whenever you feel overwhelmed by whatever it is you have set out to achieve, read this list over and over again to demonstrate to yourself that you are an extremely competent and successful woman.

Whatever you do, take time over completing this chart. This is important planning for your ideal future we're talking about here, so dedicate some quiet time when you won't be disturbed, ensure you are in an environment that helps you concentrate and relax – and have fun!

PERSONAL ACTION PLAN
Life Area: Finances

Vision statement:

Goal 1:
_____

Time-frame:

Potential challenge(s) that may prevent me achieving this goal:

Ways to overcome such challenge(s):

Goal 2:
_____

Time-frame:

Potential challenge(s) that may prevent me achieving this goal:

Ways to overcome such challenge(s):

Goal 3:
_____

Time-frame:

Potential challenge(s) that may prevent me achieving this goal:

Ways to overcome such challenge(s):

Task 1:

Deadline:

Task 2:

Deadline:

Task 3:

Deadline:

Task 4:

Deadline:

Task 5:

Deadline:

Task 6:

Deadline:

Personal strengths related to this life area
(include specific examples where possible):

1.

2.

3.

4.

Achievements in this particular life area that you are
especially proud of:

1.

2.

3.

4.

Earn more

You rarely find men underestimating their worth as much as women tend to do. Indeed, I've come across numerous examples where the most incompetent, ineffective men have held quite senior positions of power and authority, all the time believing that they were adding value to their organisations. In fact what was happening was that their ineptitude was being covered up by any number of highly efficient, skilful women – from PAs to junior executives. Yet more often than not, these women would deny that they had the ability to command much higher status, higher-paid jobs by failing to apply for promotion. Aside from the ridiculousness of such a situation, it's a scandalous fact that in this day and age women doing a job still earn less than their male equivalent. A 1999 United Nations report revealed that women continue to be paid around 80 per cent of the hourly wage of their male counterparts. We women have to take some responsibility for this. According to 1999 MORI research on behalf of the Women's Unit, women regard the income/pay gap as 'an unavoidable consequence of time away from the workplace to raise children', which makes no sense for the many women who do not, or will not, have such dependants. If we desire to change this situation, and the fact that society places less value on jobs that are predominantly held by females, we each need to upgrade our belief in our own self-worth.

While keeping more of what you earn is the key to financial security, nevertheless there is some truth in the maxim 'two live as cheaply as one', and having to manage on one income may highlight the need to value yourself more highly. If you suspect that your skills are being undervalued, there has never been a more pressing time for you to increase your income. One way of doing this is to apply for jobs that are attractive to you and would pay you more. You should seriously look at this option if, after working out what you realistically need to live a comfortable lifestyle (having made some headway into radically pruning your outgoings) you recognise that your current salary is insufficient and is unlikely to be increased at your current place of employment to any substantial degree. If you know you have portable skills that are in high demand by employers, this is an immediately attractive proposition. However, you might also use the focus of higher earnings to motivate you to learn the skills you would need to attract a bigger salary in the medium to long-term future.

Your other option is to ask for more money from your present employer. Here are some tips on how to succeed:

- Be quite clear about precisely what it is you want before you approach your boss. Do your homework. If possible, find out what is the current market rate and/or salary scale offered by your company for the job you are doing. You have to be confident about your personal worth before you can expect anyone else to be. But also be wary about unreasonably pricing yourself out of the market.

- Come up with four to six specific examples of how you add value to your organisation over and above the stated job requirements. If you have been responsible – preferably wholly – for a successful project or task, don't be afraid to say so. Believe me, few men would shy away from blowing their own trumpets, which is why they tend to rise faster through the corporate ranks.

- Think in advance about all the reasons why your company might object to paying you more, and have concrete answers ready. Don't just talk abstractly – be specific. Use your value-added examples to persuade them otherwise.

- Practice talking yourself 'up' rather than talking yourself 'down', particularly if you are applying for a promotion in order to get a higher salary. A friend of mine who has a background in politics is often asked why few women are active in this field, even at local level. She cites the case of what happens when such individuals are asked to sit on the sewage committee of their local authority – the sort of first-rung activity that fledgling politicians have to undertake. She says that in her experience women rarely get even this far since they get caught up in internally debating whether they have sufficient qualifications or will understand the technology or terminology whereas the male candidates say to themselves, 'Hey, I go to the toilet' and step forward with confidence.

- Arrange a mutually convenient time to speak to the relevant person in your organisation (a decision maker wherever possible) and let them know that increasing your salary is the topic on the agenda. That way they can't fob you off with, 'I wasn't expecting this. I'll have to go away and think about it.'

- Do whatever works for you to ensure you come across in your meeting as calm, cool and determined. I find that wearing a suit in my favourite colour – red – does the trick for me. Not only am I physically comfortable in it, but psychologically I feel dynamic and unstoppable. If you dress for success you'll embody the sort of confidence and power associated with successful people – the very people that companies are desperate to attract and retain.

- Be aware of what happens to your voice when you get nervous. Do what seasoned public speakers do. Slow down your speech, smile and take a few deep, calming breaths. To an onlooker this is indicative of a person in control of the situation. Do not get panicked into talking too fast, too loudly – or too much. Outline what you want as clearly, calmly and succinctly as possible and then shut up. Don't try and anticipate what the other person is going to say or raise objections before they do, as in 'I know the company has a policy of only offering 3 per cent annual salary increases but . . .' Listen to what your boss, or whoever you are meeting with, has to say and calmly reply using examples of why you believe you should be more generously rewarded. Also listen to the exact nature of their dissent. Do they consider that you lack experience or need a certain kind of training? Ask if they would be prepared to help develop you professionally. By saying yes, they are demonstrating that they value you as an employee.

- Avoid making threats or snap decisions. Look for a compromise. If no extra money is forthcoming now, when might the situation change? Agree on a firm date when this subject can be reviewed again. In the meantime, might the company agree to other benefits like reduced hours, rewards like paying for your gym membership, or allowing you to work from home a couple of days a week?

- Finally, if you end the meeting feeling you have not accomplished your goal, take time to ask yourself:

a) whether your company really values you as much as you deserve to be valued and

b) whether you need to do more to enhance your professional standing. For example, what hard and soft skills do you need to develop?

When you have weighed up the situation, then and only then decide on whether to look around for another, better-paid position or stay and implement any recommendations made about developing your employability.

Future planning

You may be young(ish), fit, employable and confident of your ability to earn good money for years yet, but that should not blind you to the need to plan for an equally fulfilling and secure future. This involves reviewing your pension provision and health and any other insurances. It is not possible in such a book as this, nor would it be advisable since I don't claim to be a financial expert, to offer you exact advice on your economic circumstances. They are unique to you and need to be talked through with an appropriate professional. Suffice it to say that as a woman who may be single for an indefinite period and therefore one with no means of support other than herself, it is vital that you examine your pension arrangements so that you secure an income that takes you into retirement well above the basic state pension which – on its own – would probably involve you in a dramatic lowering of living standards.

Similarly, you may have enjoyed good health for the whole of your life so far, but most of us are prone to various lifestyle or genetically linked ailments that, without prompt specialist attention, can severely affect our standard of life.

Please don't delay investigating how you will stand at retirement age or if you are suddenly faced with a major illness. No matter how small our income, we can all find some tiny sacrifice to make now to ensure that the dreams we have for ourselves as confident, independent and fulfilled single women (temporarily or permanently) are supported as far as possible by the wise investments we are making in our health and financial wellbeing.

Getting help

As I stated earlier, there's never been a better time to find the help you need to establish good money management. Don't rely on family and friends, no matter how well-meaning, to give you advice on handling your finances when there's a wealth of expert information around – much of it free. Check out:

- Your local library or bookstore for the latest books available on managing money successfully.
- The Internet (see my advice on links on p. 133).
- Advisers working for the bank or other financial institution which is handling your money.
- Magazine and newspaper articles written by experts, which have money management sections, some geared specifically to women.
- Seminars and workshops organised through your local authority or a private organisation run to help individuals develop good personal financial management.

We're now going to review a subject that so many books on being single ignore or gloss over (as indeed they do about money) – sex. So, you've 'washed that man right out of your hair', as the song goes, taken a more realistic view of what relationships mean at the beginning of the twenty-first century, got to grips with a positive mental attitude, developed a really wonderful social life, found a form of passion through your work and are engaging in effective money management. But sometimes you still crave a hug from a man. Or an orgasm. Let's now address how you can cope physically without a regular partner.

7

Sex and Intimacy

'The most consistent sex will be your love affair with yourself.'
Betty Dodson, Ph.D., *Sex for One – The Joy of Selfloving*

Simply because you sleep with a man every night doesn't mean your sex life is active – or satisfying. But feeling deprived of something that was once readily available to you (even if you didn't always take advantage of that fact) has a variety of effects on women. Consider these real-life examples:

Erin and her live-in boyfriend didn't have sex for the last year they were together because she lost her respect for him. When they split up, her sex drive was already low, although every so often she would get a sexual urge and find that she'd been walking around the supermarket, noticing men's bums.

Carnal relations between Jemma and her husband ended the moment she fell pregnant with her daughter, and she estimates that she had sex only once with him in the subsequent five years. This prompted her to start one of the affairs that still continue now she is divorced. This lover is one of several men that Jemma currently sees on an ad hoc basis. Some of them are sexual partners, others provide companionship and other kinds of support.

The sexual side of Sandy's life had died sometime before her husband of ten years walked out on her for another woman. However, just a few months into her enforced separation, Sandy has no desire to get involved physically with anyone. She wisely recognises that she needs to deal with the pain and shock of his betrayal before she can even begin to relate to another man in a way that would be meaningful to them both.

Lorna, on the other hand, found that she was literally climbing the walls with frustration the moment she became a single woman, despite having rejected the sexual advances of her husband for the latter part of her marriage. She didn't have long to wait. A bubbly, attractive, intelligent woman in her early forties, Lorna had been propositioned by work contacts many times during her fifteen-year-long marriage, and has a natural tendency to attract men like iron filings to a magnet. With the plethora of Internet chat lines and dating services now available, many of them specifically geared towards sexual encounters rather than socialising or romance, Lorna was aware that casual sex was there for the asking. However, she found that what she really craved was intimacy – an issue that many single women have to come to terms with. Her attitude now?

> There were any number of men I picked up to whom I casually said: 'I really fancy it, fuck me', and most of them were only too happy to oblige. But when the emptiness inside me persisted, I realised that I was getting my sexual and emotional needs mixed up. I really wanted someone to love me, someone I could wake up with in the mornings who would cuddle me in a caring way. Not to wake up with some stranger, as I so often did, who couldn't get out of the house fast enough.

Lorna now has a mutually agreeable arrangement with a close

male friend. Neither of them has any current ties, nor do they wish to have any other kind of relationship with each other since their values in life are very different. But this understanding allows Lorna to have regular sex with a man she is fond of, and with whom she feels a more intimate connection than with a total stranger. Richard has even been known to drive the eighty-mile round trip to give Lorna a big hug (because, for her, being on the receiving end of the male variety is very different to what she feels when being hugged by a female friend!) when she has needed one. She, in turn, is there for Richard day and night, and has counselled him through various painful break-ups with his girl-friends as and when this was required.

This kind of contract is one option for single women looking for sex, which avoids the risks associated with promiscuity. To be blunt about it, sex is available to any woman who wants it and is prepared to take that gamble with her physical, emotional and even spiritual wellbeing. After all, we live alongside those who make up almost half the population, and who are reputed to think about sex every five minutes – men. Age has nothing to do with it. The oldest woman I interviewed for this book, Sheila aged fifty-nine, told me:

> I could get sex any time I wanted, even now, because I'm one of the few women I know who is quite predatory with men. Sure, I could always find someone, and at one time in my life had a repertoire of chaps who fulfilled this purpose.

But, as she goes on to explain, in terms similar to those of Lorna, it's rarely sex alone that women find satisfactory:

> For me it has to be more than the physical act; more than physical sexual satisfaction. I don't believe many women can separate sex and lust from love in the way that men can. The vast majority of women don't just want sex in bed, they're looking for emotional involvement.

Although it may not be universally true, Sheila has highlighted the essential difference between men and women. Many males can separate the emotional from the sexual which is why they can have casual sex outside of marriage while still loving their wives, and fail to understand how their women feel threatened by this dalliance. Women, on the other hand, have a tendency to blur the boundaries between their physical needs and emotional fulfilment. Yet it's important to separate the two, because if it's the latter you are looking for while indulging in casual sex then you're likely to be left feeling empty and dissatisfied.

For many women sex is a sensual, tender experience in which – for it to be at all fulfilling – there needs to be some measure of intimacy between the individuals involved. Affection and sensitivity towards each other's emotional needs play a major role. But both sexual satisfaction and true intimacy is available to you right now, with no danger of contracting a sexually transmitted disease or unwanted pregnancy – or waking up in the morning alongside someone you don't know very well and probably wouldn't like if you did. It is the safest sex there is and it's called masturbation.

Rather than being the sad, sinful or depraved act that it has been made out to be, masturbating can be an expression of the love affair you are being urged to have with yourself. Indeed, not only is masturbation a wonderful form of relief from sexual frustration, but it will enhance this period of growth and development that you are currently experiencing. This is an opportunity to learn how to pleasure yourself so that when you choose to invite a man into your life you'll be able to communicate to him how to enhance your sensual life (a term I much prefer to the colder, more impersonal 'sex life').

Being sensual with yourself has multiple advantages over the situation many women in relationships find themselves in. You don't have to feel frustrated when you want sex, and he doesn't either; nor do you have to endure the indignity of a lover coming too fast, rolling over and falling asleep. You can take yourself to orgasm, or not, as it suits you. Many women have told me that they feel pressured into climaxing every time they make love with their partners. This Western male obsession with orgasms is another illustration of the extent to which success, performance and achieving goals are considered more important than just *being* and having fun. In Eastern philosophies the focus is largely on the quality of the experience, as you will realise if you have ever studied tantric sex or discovered the joys, as I have, of a Hindu lover.

Masturbation allows you to take full control of your experience rather than have a man dictate the place, sexual position, length of duration and what sex aids you use, if any. Touching yourself becomes another example of doing what you want, when you want, with the one person in the world who should matter to you above any other – yourself.

So – the $64,000 question: What is your attitude towards masturbation? More importantly, if your attitude is a negative one, how can you overcome this barrier to develop yourself as a sensual individual open to the pleasures of solo sex, thereby raising your sexual self-esteem? Again, we have the Church and male moralists in society to thank for the fact that, until relatively recently, masturbation has not just had a bad press, but practically no press at all. That masturbation is a taboo subject is, at last, changing. One on-line bookstore I tried threw up forty-three titles when I input the search word 'masturbation', including a complete guide to vibrators, essays on self-pleasuring written by men and women, a collection of women's sexual fantasies and even one on the 'Historical, literary and artistic discourses of autoeroticism'.

However, some pretty damning misconceptions abound, many of which would be laughable if they didn't result in so many women feeling inhibited and reluctant to experiment with this solitary pleasure. Men may joke today that masturbating regularly is likely to cause them to go blind, but this was only one of the erroneous beliefs perpetuated throughout the nineteenth century – even by the medical profession who, you would have thought, should have known better. Touching yourself intimately was said to result in all sorts of horrific physical and psychological illnesses, from hand warts and acne to sterility and lunacy. The latter assertion was based on the observation made by doctors that individuals locked up in mental institutions – with no opportunity for any other kind of sexual relief – masturbated a lot. Women were even terrorised into believing that their babies would be born deformed if they masturbated during pregnancy.

Even forty years on from the so-called sexual revolution of the 1960s, women confess to receiving negative childhood messages about masturbation which, for years, detrimentally affected their attitudes towards sexual desire and even their personal acceptance of their bodies. Their memories of being found enjoying this early type of sexual experience include being slapped across the head, having their hands tied behind their backs in order to stop them touching their private parts, and being called 'a dirty little cow'.

Yet fantasising, being intimate with your own body, gaining pleasure from solo sex and bringing yourself to climax are all natural, positive and self-loving acts. So, too, is feeling incredibly horny by looking at men (or women, according to your pre-ference). At any time, you can choose to see your sexual urges in a positive light, as does Erin, rather than reminding you of lack. She says:

> I think it's good to see the funny side of one's sexual urges. Mine remind me that I'm a woman and a sexual being. So occasionally when I lie in bed and feel really horny I tell myself that it's because I'm a really sexy woman. That's a good way to feel, rather than thinking 'I'm feeling frustrated'.

The clitoral truth

Masturbation is not a second-rate substitute for couples sex. As psychologist and sex therapist at the University of California Medical Center in San Francisco, Lonnie Garfield Barbach, points out in her book, *For Yourself: The Fulfilment of Female Sexuality*, 'Physiologically, an orgasm is an orgasm, whether it occurs during masturbation, intercourse, oral (sex) or any other form of stimulation.'

Indeed, for many women masturbation is the *only* way they have found to achieve orgasm. A 1972 study conducted on behalf of the Playboy Foundation by professional sex therapists in the United States found that 47 per cent of women married for an average of fifteen years did not regularly experience orgasm while having sex with their husbands. The situation was found to be even more dire for single women, of whom only 30 per cent were consistently orgasmic with a partner.

It took the publication in the 1960s of sex experts William H. Masters and Virginia E. Johnson's studies into the human sexual response to prove that more women not only achieved orgasm through masturbation, but that they could achieve multiple orgasms as long as the stimulation continued. How little we have understood female sexual behaviour until relatively recently. Only a decade previously, when researcher Alfred C. Kinsey disclosed publicly that 14 per cent of women interviewed achieved multiple orgasms, it was suggested that this was impossible.

Making love alone

As stated earlier, there are any number of specialist books, written by qualified sex therapists and other knowledgeable individuals, available to you if you would like to further explore the mechanics of masturbation and how to bring yourself to orgasm – perhaps for the first time in your life. And, remember, one of the advantages of masturbating when you are single is that you can enjoy it as often as you like without being concerned with offending your male partner or having him feel threatened by your desire to pleasure yourself. While some men undoubtedly get a thrill from watching a woman play with herself, many feel that it's an indictment on their ability to satisfy her. Plus, because masturbation has been shrouded in secrecy for centuries, particularly for women because our genitals are less prominent than men's, you may feel too vulnerable to share this activity with a partner.

The ways in which we each prefer to be stimulated are as diverse as our choices of food or fashion. However, if you are willing – and I sincerely hope you are – to engage in sexual intimacy through masturbation, here are some suggestions as to how to enhance this experience, including experimenting with the type of sensory stimulation you respond to best:

- If you are a visually oriented woman, you might like to check out various forms of erotic art or pornography – either through pictures, magazines, videos or on the Internet. There's no need to feel worried or confused about your sexual orientation if you find looking at women's bodies as much, if not more, of a turn on as looking at men's. A sexy female body in a pose that does not demean women – as, unfortunately, much of hardcore pornography does – may well give you an erotic thrill and that is perfectly natural.

- Alternatively, you may respond better to sounds, and there are many instrumental tracks with pulsating or soothing beats that can be very sexy. I find Middle Eastern music, the sort that belly dancers gyrate to, a huge turn on.

- Smell might be more important to you and there are a number of traditionally sensuous aromas available as incense sticks, oils for burning or creams and oils for massaging into your body. My favourite scents include musk, vanilla, ylang ylang and jasmine. Try exploring various essential oil ranges to see what sensual selections they offer. Or find an experienced aromatherapist who will make up a personal blend for you.

- Many women, myself included, find using their fingers to stimulate their clitoris less satisfactory than using a vibrator. If you feel too inhibited to visit a sex shop (and there are some high-street outlets which are less tacky and safer for a woman to enter alone than their back-street counterparts) that doesn't matter. Vibrators are sold as tools for stimulating acupressure points or easing stiff and sore muscles, so you will probably find what you need in a department store or large pharmacy. Or try mail order. Using a lubricating gel rather than relying on your own natural juices enhances the vibratory experience.

• Indulge your fantasies. You have been equipped with your very own sexual theatre – your imagination – so do use it. In the privacy of your bedroom, with none of the distractions linked to sharing it with another person, you can totally concentrate on what turns you on. If you have not experimented with this form of erotic response before and are concerned about what is 'normal', then you might like to explore written compilations of other women's sexual fantasies, such as *My Secret Garden* by Nancy Friday.

Energy refocus

You may have read what I have written so far and decided that there's not an hailstone's hope in hell that you will be masturbating with abandon tonight – or any other night. And that's your prerogative. However, sexual energy needs to be focused elsewhere if it is not to become repressed, thereby adding to your stress levels. If you are resistant to touching yourself intimately you might choose to do a work-out at the gym, go for a long walk, take an invigorating shower (well, it's a popular method in all those single sex schools), clean the house from top to bottom or get gardening. Just be aware that your sexual energy will not dissipate simply by trying to ignore it. I would suggest you actively choose to redirect this powerful force through (preferably) physical channels, in order to ensure it is being expressed in some other form.

In answer to the question: 'How do you cope with your sexual desires without a regular partner?', Harriet answered:

I don't find that's a problem for me. Whenever I get 'urges' I have a warm bath, relax, pamper myself and read a good book. I just don't dwell on it. I have a list of daily goals that are so compelling and challenging that every moment is already accounted for. By the time I've accomplished them I'm too exhausted to think about sex – there are so many other things I can do to take my mind off it. I certainly wouldn't be interested in casual sex, as I believe it is more rewarding to wait for the right person to come into your life. I would never want to wake up and feel ashamed of myself.

Like Harriet, you may have reached a stage where your sexual desires have 'shut down' and you are focusing your mind on other matters – your children, your work, your self-development – so that you feel no need to masturbate or seek sexual or sensual expression with anyone. I, and many of the women I spoke with, have experienced the same. But you may be reassured to know that, no matter how long this period of contented celibacy has been, your sex drive will switch back on when you meet a desirable man, someone with whom you share sexual chemistry.

Learning to love and pleasure your body contributes hugely to your self-esteem because you are engaging in an important aspect of self-love. And the greater you love yourself, the more you will be able to experience true intimacy with any future man. But there's another form of intimacy that has nothing to do with sexual expression: it's the intimacy which, as a single parent, you will be sharing in a perhaps more challenging way with your child now that you no longer have a partner to share the responsibilities with.

As I pointed out in the introduction, this isn't an extensive or detailed chapter on single parenthood – there are many books out there that can help you with the various issues you and your children may be facing. But I wanted to acknowledge, through the experiences of several women I spoke to about this subject, that being a single parent can be a life-enhancing experience, just as being a single woman can be. Whether you choose to believe this is up to you.

Two's company

There are any number of ways in which you can immerse yourself in the negative messages and fallacies bandied about regarding single parenthood. These include paying attention to the out-pourings of some politicians obsessed with 'family values' (whatever they may be), and getting too caught up in the sensationalism of television programmes out to portray all single parents as irresponsible, unmarried mothers, who are dragging up a generation of disaffected youth. In my view, this is just another example of societal misogyny, given that 91 per cent of the single parent families in the UK are headed by women. I'm not intending to add to this doom-mongering and negativity here.

Within that supposedly homogenous mass labelled 'single parents' there are women whose partners have died, leaving them with youngsters to raise single-handedly, women who are separated or divorced, whose children live with them and who rarely – if ever – see their fathers, or those who have chosen to give birth or adopt a child outside of a regular partnership. Single parenthood takes courage. But the rewards for that courage can be amazing, once the initial shock and uncertainty has been overcome and some readjustment made to the family lifestyle.

I conclude this chapter by exploring three key issues of successful single parenting:

1. How to ensure that your relationship with your children is mutually satisfying and enhances the personal growth of all concerned.
2. Why it is important to offer your children the benefits of a male role model, even if he is not their father.
3. Why you need to focus appropriately on your needs as well as theirs.

Let me say at the outset that I have not been a single parent; I left my children in the care of my ex-husband when they were fourteen and twelve years old. Having never been particularly maternal, I found to my delight that I had a better relationship with them outside of the family home than I did when I was living with them. They are wonderful, well-balanced, mature young people of whom I'm immensely proud – and I acknowledge that much of the credit for that fact goes to their father and the way he has guided and supported them over the past few years. But I claim credit, too, not only for having helped them develop into independent and self-confident individuals in their formative years, but also for the fact that I took great pains to ensure that their father and I had an amicable parting – and that they saw that this was so.

You might expect me to say this, given my personal circumstances, but I have never believed that divorce per se is responsible for messing with children's heads and ruining their lives. It is the quality of the relationship which the separated parents have, which matters most. A mutually respectful, friendly exchange between you and your children's father maintains some sort of support structure that youngsters need when their parents split up. However, I would be the first to recognise that I cannot talk about single parenthood from anything other than a theoretical perspective. Which is why the issues that we will be exploring will be illustrated by the real-life case histories of three women I interviewed for this book.

There are, of course, many other issues concerning single parenthood that limited space precludes me from covering – such as childcare, your work life, having a discreet sex life and managing with less money (although I hope the previous chapter on finances will help you with that). That is why I urge you to research specialist books on this subject, or find a local or Internet discussion group to help guide and support you as necessary.

This wonderful life

Many single parents say that their relationship with their children turned out to be much closer, easier and hence more satisfactory than they had thought it would be. Human beings have a wonderful way of pulling together through challenging situations, forgetting their own, petty needs and issues in an effort to ensure 'the family' or even 'the nation' thrives.

Single parenting can demonstrate to you, and your child, just how strong, resourceful and resilient you really are. This fact was highlighted in a recent UK Sunday supplement article in which four very different women talked about how bringing up their children alone radically changed their lives for the better. One of them was quoted as saying, 'Being a (single) mother is the hardest job I've ever done, but I wouldn't give my daughter back for the world.'

Because it can be so challenging, sometimes pushing you to your limits physically and emotionally, it is easy to give in to your child's frequently unreasonable demands. Like singleness generally, being a single parent doesn't have to be worse than being in a parental partnership, it's just different. And because of this you may need to adopt new strategies. This was the lesson Caroline learned when her husband of twelve years suddenly decided that his secretary could satisfy his personal needs as well as his professional ones, and he abandoned his family. She takes up the story:

Brian didn't just cut me out of his life when he left home, but also our three children – at that time five, seven and ten years of age. I completely fell to pieces and focused only on the downsides, including the fact that I would have no time to myself. I worried constantly about money and felt very isolated and lonely. Many of our mutual friends found the situation too embarrassing for them to deal with and so 'dropped me' from their lives too. Suddenly, I realised I had no adult support since my parents were both dead, and I became concerned about whether I was up to making all the household decisions when I'd relied so heavily in the past on Brian.

It seemed easier just to let the kids do what they wanted and I recognise now that this was one of the side-effects of my depression; I was so wrapped up in feeling sorry for myself that I didn't have the time or energy to discipline them. Luckily, I soon snapped out of that when their school reports alerted me to the fact that my three little angels were very quickly becoming unruly, unpopular and out of control.

That's when I had to trawl the very depths of my energy resources and began to discipline them more firmly. They say necessity is the mother of invention and this was certainly the case – to the benefit of us all. I told the children that I needed them to help me more around the house and to their credit they rose to this superbly. Even the youngest one didn't want to be left out. I rewarded them by involving them in minor decision making, such as what colour we should repaint the hall and whether to buy a Golden Labrador or West Highland Terrier. Brian had always hated pets, but I missed having a dog in the house, since I grew up with them.

I considered this increased negotiation to be an apprenticeship for my children's adult lives. They learned that money did not grow on trees and became incredibly creative and resourceful at getting their material needs met, rather than simply asking Daddy for money.

My children have suffered neither from the various, and often contradictory, rules and restrictions imposed on them in two-parent households, nor from the freedom and lack of limitations that you sometimes see when one parent is having to bring them up alone. That was a fine line for me to walk sometimes. I have learned to regard myself as a leader to my children, someone who encourages them to engage in open and honest communication, genuinely seeks their input and is sensitive to their opinions, no matter how immature they might seem. I found that when I was honest with them – not being able to afford to take them to a theme park or whatever – they respected me for that. I never said a word against their father, but did everything in my power to create a stable and nurturing home for them. I sincerely believe that if you expect your child to grow up to be a mature, balanced, respectful individual, then they need to see you acting in that way – not some vengeful, erratic fishwife.

If I were to offer advice to women who find themselves in a similar situation, I would say that you must maintain a degree of authority. By demonstrating to your children that you are still in charge, this will help them feel secure and rooted. Most of all, don't rob them of their precious childhood by making them your parent, peer or partner. Firm guidance will help them see that they need to maintain control of their own impulses in life, and will ensure they grow up knowing how to make wise choices.

In order to enhance your children's personal growth as well as your own, it's important not to make them the centre of your life or to use them as a prop for your unhappiness. Recently I was in a restaurant where a single mother and her three-year-old son occupied the next table. You would have thought that the boy was the King of England, the way he was being treated. Oliver, a prime candidate for later therapy if ever I saw one, was given licence to choose his own meal, and his mother fussed over his food and the fact that he obviously didn't want to eat it, to the extent that nothing on her own plate was touched. She talked to him and expected him to make choices as if he were an adult, when he was little more than a toddler. Her approach, therefore, was totally inappropriate. This woman used emotional blackmail to try and get her child to eat, almost suggesting that Mummy's life would fall apart if Oliver didn't make her happy by finishing his meal. Frankly, it was all rather nauseating to watch.

If you find yourself in need of a friend and confidante, find an adult one. It's good to encourage children to take a junior partnership role in your household, but not to treat them as equal – or even superior – partners. And this advice holds true irrespective of whether your family has single or dual parents.

Role models

Having a man in a youngster's life in undeniably beneficial, as Hesta found when she got married for the second time to Martin, when her son Ian was fourteen years old:

> A male role model finished Ian off in a way I never could. Martin, who was some years younger than me, taught him things like how to shake hands and how to read the body language of girls in a disco. Even though things didn't work out for Martin and me – and I didn't marry him to provide Ian with a father figure – I'm immensely grateful to my second husband for the male guidance he gave my son.

Jemma's daughter, Claire, was nine years old when her parents divorced. Jemma has seen a number of her divorced female friends enter inappropriate relationships or, worse, get remarried, to men they didn't really love, in order to provide their children with a male role model. Jemma's solution was not to marry again but to encourage her daughter to still see a long-standing lover, even after Jemma and Frank ended their relationship:

> Claire had become very fond of Frank, and he of her, so when we broke up after two and a half years together, I discussed with him the importance of him still being available to her, particularly since she had lost all contact with her natural father.
> Frank was an incredible influence on Claire as she grew up from being a child to a young woman. They would do all sorts of exciting things together, like white-water rafting – all the physical and sporting activities that I've never been into. Frank was able to offer Claire a perspective on men that was invalu-

able to her as a confused teenager. He was even able to persuade her, in a way that even I, as her mother, couldn't on issues such as not to lose her virginity to some good looking but otherwise cavalier and immature sports jock.

It may be a brother, your own father, or a male family friend whom you trust implicitly. If you can, without looking to replace their natural father, encourage your children to have a mentor-type relationship with a significant role model who will be a constant in their lives for some time, particularly if their birth father is unwilling or unable to be available to them.

No one doubts that a mother's love and guidance is vital for her children's emotional and psychological, as well as physical, wellbeing. But to enjoy a well-rounded perspective on life they – and you – may find it beneficial to have a male role model to look up to and confide in.

Your needs

The great Swiss psychologist Carl Gustav Jung once said, 'Nothing has a stronger influence psychologically on their environment and especially on their children than the unlived life of the parent.' This is why you need to focus appropriately on your needs, as a unique human being, as well as directly on theirs. Your wellbeing is vital to the benefit of your child, therefore it is important to be kind and generous-hearted to yourself. Stop giving yourself a hard time about what you think your children are being deprived of, and focus on creating a stable and nurturing environment for you all.

Many adults, the children of warring parents themselves, who endured years of living in hostile and dysfunctional homes, say that there are worse things in life than divorce, or losing a father who wasn't there for them much anyway because he spent long hours at work. You now have a wonderful opportunity to develop a fulfilling relationship with your children which, as you will no doubt be aware by now, requires you to develop a truly fulfilling relationship with yourself – the subject of this entire book.

Here's 44-year-old Shona's advice:

I had for so long put my own life on hold for the sake of my husband and children, that it took me a long time to rediscover who I was after Ken died. I had always believed he would be around to look after us, so it came as a huge shock to find that, not only did I have my kids to look after, but I also had to relearn how to nurture myself.

I didn't do a very good job of the latter until my teenage daughter, who has always been mature beyond her years, told me that I wasn't doing anyone any favours by martyring myself, and wasn't it about time I started paying more attention to *me*? She pointed out, quite rightly, that in just a few years she and her twin brother would be leaving for university or even to travel abroad for a year or two, and that if I didn't start focusing more on *my* life and *my* needs, it would be like experiencing another death. Kerry, not the most altruistic of individuals, told me that she didn't want to feel guilty about leaving – so wasn't it about time I got my life back?

That gave me the jolt I needed. I realised I wanted another adult in the house so I decided to rent out the spare room, which also helped us out financially. Although local eyebrows were raised at first, Bob turned out to be a godsend. He hadn't wanted to uproot his children who were at really good schools 200 miles away from where he now worked. But he was sick of living in hotels part of the week. So he stayed with us from Monday evenings to Friday mornings and went back to his family at weekends. It was nice having a man around the house again and I even became quite friendly on the phone with his wife.

I think a lot of single mothers set themselves up to be self-sacrificial lambs, but even if you are tied up with your children, it's important to find the time to do nice things just for yourself – to remember what it's like to be a woman and not just a mother.

I used the extra money that Bob's rent brought in to have regular aromatherapy massages, attend to my greying hair every six weeks at the hairdressers, and to take a language class and word-processing skills course, so that I might shortly re-enter the workplace. I also co-founded a local support group for single parents, and we've set up a number of initiatives that mean it's not all about talk and navel-gazing, but about ways to help each other practically too.

Concentrating more on my needs has made me a nicer person to be around and that has benefited the children. I know they respect me more now, because for probably the first time in my life I respect, admire and love myself.

Making space in your life for you, and not just everyone else, demonstrates that you think of yourself and your needs as important. Undoubtedly it is more challenging for single parents, as opposed to single women, to get to know what their needs are because of maternal feelings of guilt and having less time to devote to just oneself. However, if you can think of selfishness (as opposed to being self-centred) as a positive, rather than an undesirable, trait then you will soon discover that others begin to treat you, as Shona found, with greater respect and admiration. This includes any man that you may decide to welcome into your life.

8

The Choice of Loving

'Men and women who know themselves will stand an excellent chance of selecting a mate well suited to them.'
Neil Clark Warren, Ph.D., *Two Dates or Less.*

In the 1980s film *War Games* the US Chiefs of Staff are forced to rethink their defence strategy and training when a large percentage of officers required to set off nuclear missiles fails to do so, even when they are led to believe that Russia is attacking their country. When they were faced with the prospect of setting off a holocaust, even the rigorous military training of these men could not override their natural, human aversion to being responsible for the deaths of hundreds of thousands of people.

In business, too, what is thought to work in theory often does not turn out to be successful in practice. For example, companies can work for years developing a product or service that seems like a great idea, but in actual fact turns out to be a monumental flop because the public just doesn't buy it.

While some of you may find that your experience of singleness and the self-empowerment you achieve in that period attracts someone who undoubtedly is your soulmate, others may go through a series of transitional arrangements. These 'growing relationships', are an invaluable 'reality check'. They offer you the opportunity to test and see whether the empowering attitudes, beliefs and behaviour you have developed during periods of single life are really embedded, and thus can help you steer a positive course through life, even in the most challenging circumstances. The majority of us want to be in a significant relationship – it feels natural to pair up, even if that isn't officially recognised in the form of a marriage. Our genetic predisposition to procreate – or at least be in a situation where we could if we wanted to – is unlikely to be shifted overnight. Yes, some women I have spoken with have implied that they intend to spend the rest of their lives being single. But upon probing deeper, most admit that they avoid relationships because they prefer not to risk being hurt again. In many cases they remain single more from a fear of the challenges that relating presents, rather than because they are opting to be permanently by themselves. In my experience, most women who want one, find a man to share their life with.

Developing a really fulfilling single life, and desiring to enjoy a significant relationship, are not mutually exclusive. Indeed, I like to think of them as different steps to learn in the dance of life so that your repertoire and sense of enjoyment is as wide as possible. It may well be that as you work through the lessons in this book someone comes into your life who seems absolutely wonderful and perfect for you. That's certainly happened recently to a number of women I know who have been long-term and very happily single – two of whom I interviewed for this book. And, ironically, it has happened to me. Whether these are true soul-mates or 'transitional men', only time will tell.

Everyone said I was tempting fate by writing a book about being contentedly single. Halfway through this project I began a relationship with a man who – to all intents and purposes – is my emotional, intellectual, financial and spiritual equal. We even share a birthday. I call him my 'walking list' because he so perfectly embodies all the criteria I had identified as desiring in a life partner. Rather than embarrassing me, given that I am setting myself up as an expert on contented singleness, his appearance in my life has been a blessing, enabling me to write this chapter with much more authenticity. Indeed, my focus all along has been to demonstrate how a period of solitude and getting to know yourself really well superbly equips you for an innately satisfying and fulfilling relationship with another person – but, as a life choice, not a necessity.

I know that this process does work – that of working on yourself in order to change your life for the better. By changing myself I have attracted into my life someone completely different to any man I have related to before. Whether he is simply another pit stop on my spiritual journey, or the Great Love of My Life, doesn't matter because I know that with or without him my life is pretty wonderful.

Erin has a similar, positive story to tell. She met Sean just a few months after I had interviewed her about successfully managing her single life. In less than two months they were living together and certainly seem destined to live the rest of their lives together. Frankly, given the enhanced life stage that Erin had reached, this doesn't surprise me. The quality of her relationship with Sean is a reflection of the quality of the relationship she has developed with herself. As Erin puts it:

Being on my own has taught me that first you have to grow yourself as a person and experience what it's like to be an individual. Then, when you choose to enter into a relationship, you have the maturity to allow the other person to be who they are – and that is an extremely magnetic quality.

Delighted as I am by Erin's happiness, a more instructive story to share with you, I believe, is that of Penny. This is because her much more challenging situation highlights the dangers of letting all that good work you've done on yourself be forgotten the moment a man comes into your life – as inevitably he will, should you desire it.

Penny works for an international PR firm and had organised an event in New York for one of her clients where she met David, one of the keynote speakers. Single for some years, Penny was immediately fascinated by this compelling man. He seemed to possess many of the qualities Penny admired in herself. David was independent, successful, emotionally open and fun to be with. He very much came across as the kind of man who 'owns himself'.

To cut a long story short, they began what can only be described as an email romance, the only thing available to them, given the fact that Penny lived in London, England and David in Seattle, USA. Luckily, a month or so after their initial meeting, David was due to attend a conference in England. It was during the passionate and intimate week they spent together that Penny and David fell head over heels in love with each other.

However, a relationship conducted over thousands of miles is a contradiction in terms. Both of them knew, despite David having two more business trips to make to the UK in the next few months, that if they were going to take this further than a long-distance friendship one of them would have to relocate. They decided to compromise. David invited Penny to stay with him over the summer assessing that, by the time her three-month tourist visa ran out, they would know whether they were able to live together or not. Having planned to hand in her notice in order to start work on her first novel, Penny accepted David's offer immediately. She figured that a working holiday in the United States would be a wonderful adventure, with the possibility that she and David might turn into a permanent fixture. Despite having been happily single since her divorce four years previously, Penny had given up casual dating because she wanted to meet a man with whom she could share a long-term, committed relationship.

Penny was leaving behind – ostensibly temporarily – the vibrant social life and close friendships that she had developed over the years. She no longer felt she was carrying any baggage from earlier relationships, and had worked hard to conquer her fear of loneliness, thanks to her very satisfying and successful career in public relations. Ever the optimist, Penny was convinced that she and David would soon be walking off into the sunset together – just as Erin (whom she knows casually) and Sean seemed to be doing. Having been a frequent visitor to the United States even before the break-up of her marriage, Penny had always had a penchant for American men, particularly highly intelligent, fascinating ones like David.

Within a week of Penny's arrival in Seattle, David lost his job. Instead of feeling supportive and glad that she could be there for him at this traumatic time, Penny felt cheated. She began to withdraw into herself, pining for the romance that had marked their first few months of being together. Because David was busy setting up meetings with headhunters and attending interviews, Penny was left very much to her own devices in an area she was not familiar with. Unlike New York, which she knew like the back of her hand, Seattle was unknown to Penny. Worse still, in her eyes at least, by taking the car to his appointments every day, David had left her to fend for herself in a neighbourhood of Seattle without the widespread transportation Penny was used to in London. Although Penny also lived in a city, her little house in a quiet, tree-lined road in Fulham seemed a million miles away from what she was now having to contend with.

Perceiving that David was neglecting her, Penny became more and more upset. By her own admission she was crying virtually every day. She had little or no appetite, and was having such trouble sleeping that she started taking tranquillisers. Penny constantly focused on what she had left behind – her busy professional and personal life, her family, the home she had so lovingly furnished and the funky little sports car she had such fun driving – rather than what her new life could offer. Her self-esteem took a nose dive. She began to put pressure on David to spend more time with her and, although he was understanding at first, he pointed out that this wasn't practical in the circumstances and it caused frequent arguments between them. Penny also became worried about money because she hadn't really thought through the financial implications of moving to the United States, where she was precluded from taking on any freelance work. Penny became mildly depressed and, because of that, couldn't concentrate on the outline of her novel. With little money, no job, and negativity weighing down on her like a heavy stone, Penny feared that David would think her worthless and begin a relationship with someone else.

By the time Penny, a former coaching client, called me – practically a month to the day after her arrival in Seattle – she was almost at the point of telling David she wanted to go home. He, guessing that Penny was desperately unhappy, offered to go back to live in England where he had many contacts and was confident he could find immediate employment. Penny, hugely conflicted, didn't know what to do, which is why she called me. On the one hand, she told me, this was not how she had expected her life with David to be. She particularly felt that they had settled too quickly into an established relationship when what she still wanted was the fantasy of a holiday romance. But Penny was also fearful of throwing in the towel on a cosmopolitan lifestyle and the loving relationship that she had always said she desired to find.

Had Penny come to you for support and guidance, what would you have told her? I realised I was talking to a woman completely at odds with the focused, go-getting, inspiring in-dividual that I knew. What do you think happened to change her so dramatically?

Well, to put it bluntly, Penny forgot who she was and that she, and only she, had total responsibility for her life. Indeed, Penny no longer had a life. Moving to the United States had created a vacuum in her life that she habitually looked to David to fill. Under normal circumstances he might have been willing to do that – for a time. But given the fact that he had to focus on establishing himself in his new job, he could not devote 100 per cent of his time and energy to Penny, as had been the case when he'd visited her in London. And, to be fair, he had gone out of his way to take her around his city to try and help her become oriented with this new way of life.

When you are depressed, worried, anxious, fed up, lonely or

bored it is not advisable to spend copious amounts of time going over and over the cause of your discontent, which is why I was hesitant to let Penny ramble on about how unsatisfying her life in Seattle seemed. If you want to change your present circumstances, you need to *do* something – take action to fill your life with something other than your concerns. I advised Penny to stop crying for the moon or over spilt milk and led her through a process of transformation to turn her poison into medicine. Back, in fact, to the woman that David had originally fallen in love with.

The first question I asked Penny was: What are you worried about?

She articulated that David, believing that they were the ideal couple, was putting pressure on her to sell her possessions in London and come and move permanently to Seattle to be with him. He thought that this affirmation of his commitment would help Penny feel more secure and therefore happier. It did not. She had some concerns about the long-term success of the relationship which, because of all the drama she had been putting David through, she felt uncomfortable expressing. Having spoken to a number of girlfriends in the UK about how she felt, Penny had come to the conclusion that she couldn't make a valid decision as to whether to go back to London or stay with David in the United States until her mind was on a more even keel. She needed space to think about what she really wanted. This, Penny felt, she could only do when she had returned home after her visa had run out.

In answer to the question, 'What are you worried about?' Penny told me that she was concerned that, if she sold everything in the UK and moved to Seattle, and the relationship failed at some point in the future, she would end up with no home or security – with nothing, in fact. And at the age of thirty-nine, having built up her life again after her divorce, she was reluctant to do that.

My next question to Penny was: 'What can you do to circumvent that worse case scenario?'

Penny's first reaction was, 'Nothing.' She assessed that there was nothing she could do about it if she and David were not destined to be together, correctly assessing that no one could give her a cast-iron assurance that they would love each other or want to be together forever. However, the first answer you come up with is not necessarily the right one. It is certainly not the only one. I prompted Penny to think about that question again: 'What can you do to circumvent the fear that is causing you to worry so much?' Penny thought a little more, and eventually replied, 'To rediscover the woman I really am – the one David fell in love with in the first place. A woman who, when she is in a positive life state, can handle just about anything. After all, I picked myself up and dusted myself down after my divorce and created a life for myself that was far more successful, in so many ways, than it had been when I was married.'

We agreed to work with this possibility rather than be too fatalistic about accepting whatever life decided to throw Penny's way. During this discussion, Penny mentioned that arriving in the US had caused her to feel, 'like a fish out of water'. I asked her to tell me how she could rectify that and she laughingly replied, 'Get the fish back into the bowl.' Penny was now in the right frame of mind to take the action necessary to deal realistically with her concerns.

My next question was: 'What do you need to do to get your life back, while keeping the door to your relationship open?'

Penny came up with this six-point action plan:

1. Rent or borrow a car for the two months until she was due to return to England. This would give her the freedom to explore the area David lived in, irrespective of whether he had the time to go with her or not.

2. Join the sort of professional and special interest groups that Penny would be connected with back in the UK in order to develop a social support structure.
3. Network like crazy in order to get more writing work.
4. Think about other ways in which to make money that did not involve anything illegal.
5. Set one goal – be it professional or personal – every day, and achieve it.
6. Focus her mind on enjoying a working holiday rather than obsessing about whether or not her relationship had any chance of success.

Penny had fallen into the trap that many successfully single women fall into when they meet a man who they can see themselves creating a life with. She had started to rely on this man to meet her needs when in fact she had long been accomplished at looking after herself. Our social conditioning is highly resistant to change. We need to be constantly alert for signs that we are relinquishing full responsibility for our happiness. Penny had mistakenly thought happiness to be the absence of all problems when in fact – to be realistic about it – happiness is simply realising that any problem can be solved.

Almost from the moment that Penny started to focus on the adventure and opportunities that this trip offered her, rather than concentrating solely on the likelihood of the success of this relationship, her mood lifted. As she started to feel better about herself she felt an increased sense of love and caring for David. They began to act like the adoring couple they had been when they first met. Penny, especially, found that her life outside of her relationship with David was as fulfilling as it was inside it. Her social life started to develop and, with it, opportunities to write about the many interesting experiences she came into contact with. Penny still wanted her relationship with David to work, but no longer needed it to. As she felt less desperate about it, and took control of her life in a positive, focused way, her worries eased.

It is usually the case that relating a painful experience like Penny's – outlining the pitfalls of going back into a serious relationship – is far more instructive to the rest of us than Erin's tale of 'happy ever after'. The following is a ten-point checklist to consider whenever you feel that you are losing sight of your own happiness and, more importantly, your ability to orchestrate that happiness in whichever way you choose. You might like to rewrite these points, developing them in whatever way you like, transcribing them into your journal or typing them on to a sheet of paper to be pinned up with other salutary messages and affirmations. If you keep these points in the forefront of your mind, you will ensure that your decision to love again remains an empowering life choice and not a need or an obsession.

1. Commit every day to living your life for yourself. Your self-sufficiency is a hard-won and precious inner resource – don't give it away.
2. Consider the benefits which the man entering your life is bringing to it. What trade-offs are you having to negotiate – say, between total freedom and having someone to snuggle up with at nights? Are you content with making those trade-offs, or are they eating away at your core values?
3. Be giving in your relationship by all means without necessarily expecting exactly the same in return. But balance these outgoings by giving as much time, energy and pleasure to yourself as you do to a man.
4. Do a 'spot check' every day on your ability to live with joy in your heart, particularly if you are a long-term 'what if?' worrier. Imagine that the worst has already happened and that you and your partner are no longer together. Assess the extent to which your life is still purposeful and fulfilling to you. Rectify any deficits by taking the appropriate action, such as revitalising your personal social life, taking up a new hobby or special interest, or focusing more on developing your working life.
5. Every time you slip back into thinking: 'Why isn't he doing

this for me?' consider what you would have done if you were living without him. How would you cope then? How did you cope before you met him? Whatever you expect someone else to provide for you, you can give to yourself. You might just need to apply some creative thinking as to how. Remember, expectation breeds disappointment. Learn not to expect anything from anyone except the one person you can trust totally – yourself.

6. If you find yourself putting his needs before your own, from the time you are devoting to him to the fact that you serve him better food than you would cook if you were by yourself, then consider this: Generally speaking the scraps in any household go into the bin or the dog. Is that how you think of yourself?

7. Ask yourself every morning: 'What brings me joy?' Then seek it out. He may have become a significant part of your pleasure but never let him be the only source of happiness in your life. Joy belongs to you, no human being ever does.

8. Self-esteem is a compilation of all the beliefs you have about yourself. Watch for ways in which he is causing you to get locked into false beliefs about yourself in ways such as criticising you, nitpicking, putting you down in front of other people, thinking he can get away with treating you in a cavalier fashion, or in any number of other ways in which men chip away at a woman's self-confidence. You've already had to overcome centuries of social conditioning, parenting, media messages and other negative contributions to your self-image. Why are you adding to the list?

9. Never forget that you have always lived – and still do – with the Great Love of Your Life: yourself. 'He' is simply an added benefit.

10. No matter what challenge life presents you with, affirm every day that it is good to be alive. After all, consider the alternative!

Words of wisdom

In answer to the question, 'If you could give one piece of advice to women who find themselves unexpectedly, even uncomfortably, single – what would it be?' The women I interviewed for this book came up with a variety of positive suggestions.

JEMMA Change your environment to support the new 'you'

If yours was a live-in arrangement the first thing to do, once he's gone, is to redecorate the place. If all you can manage is to move the furniture, then do that. Eighteen months after I threw my husband out, the house was still decked out in the beiges, browns, oranges and golds that he had chosen years before. The moment I started to change my living environment I began to change. I painted, wallpapered and got rid of anything that reminded me of that relationship and immediately felt freer to commit to my new life.

I realised this was going to be traumatic for my nine-year-old daughter so I got her involved too. I suggested she look at lifestyle magazines, and rely on her innate good taste and tell me what she liked – not just for her room but the whole house. Together we decked out the place in really dramatic colours and animal prints, which we love.

If your ex didn't live-in then think about changing your fashion style or hair colour. I had my hair cut very short so that I looked physically different, to emphasise the fact that I was not the same person that I was when I was with him. Even if you have become widowed or your marriage was happier than mine, I still think it's important, when creating a new future, not to stay rooted to the past by surrounding yourself with memories.

SHEILA: Stop thinking 'If only'

Take responsibility for your life on an emotional, as well as a practical, level. Accept that this is how your life is and work with, and build on, what you have.

I've found my Buddhist practice to be enormously useful in helping me come to terms with why painful things happen. I think it's invaluable during times of immense change or grief to find a philosophy that works for you. Fear and faith can't exist in the same space – and I know which one I would rather live with.

MANDY: Find inspirational role models

There are probably loads of fascinating and inspiring characters to discover in your family, just as there are in mine. I took the focus off my newly single situation by researching our family history and discovered many adventurous ancestors who did exciting things all by themselves, in much more challenging situations than mine. That helped me realise that I, too, have a lust for life that would not suit settling down with a man and having his children. I want to travel the world and write a book. If I were in a relationship those personal commitments would be harder to negotiate.

I'm thirty-eight now and have never been married but, I discovered, one of my aunts had remained single until quite late in life, which I think is a great option. Rather than thinking of it as missing out on anything, she told me she'd had a great life with a majorly successful career and lots of travel. That's exactly what I want to be able to say when I reach her age.

SANDY: Recognise the value of professional guidance and support

I went to pieces when my husband left me for another woman and even though they meant well, my friends and family couldn't help me. None of them knew what to say or, more importantly, how to encourage me out of the pit I had sunk into. Regardless of how well meaning people are, if they haven't had professional training or first-hand experience of what you're going through, how can they offer anything other than sympathy? And I needed something more tangible than that. Plus, I'd lived away from home since I was nineteen and had always been very independent so it didn't feel right to go running back to my parents at thirty-three years of age.

I finally got myself motivated enough to seek out professional guidance and have been seeing my counsellor on and off since the separation. She explained the grieving process to me and reassured me that what I was experiencing was completely normal. We also talked about how, if I didn't work my way through the various stages and get them sorted out once and for all, I would have problems later. I suppose what was important to me was having someone I paid to listen to me, so I didn't feel guilty about taking up their time. I believe you should look upon professional counselling as an important first step in recognising that your physical and psychological good health is important.

ERIN: Do the work – then look for the mirror

Having spent time on my own and taken responsibility for my life, it's made me very aware that a characteristic that's very important to me in a future partner is someone who, too, has worked on themselves. He doesn't have to have gone on self-development courses necessarily, but he needs to own himself to the same extent I do – so that he is a mirror of myself. I like the person I am, so I'm looking for someone who is – in certain ways – quite similar to me. Opposites do attract but as a rule they don't have a lot in common, so there tends to be no longevity in those relationships.

If you are starting to look for someone similar to yourself I think that's a very good indication that you have got to the point of liking yourself. When you do meet such a person there's mutual respect. I'm quite forceful, and very forward, and not a lot of men can deal with that. But I need a ballsy guy because that's what I'm comfortable with in myself. I believe it's a good sign if you go for someone who reminds you of you.

HESTA: Acceptance is key

Accept the grieving that accompanies the loss of any important relationship, and that it's an essential part of closing the door to the past. Get people who care for you around you – family and close friends who will nurture and support you through difficult or painful times.

Don't be frightened. Just remember, there are lots of positive things to experience from every situation you find yourself in.

HARRIET: *It's never too late to share*

Don't get into unsuitable relationships just because you're afraid that, the longer you live by yourself, the harder you'll find it to share your life with someone. Loving yourself totally is like being a child with constant, free access to candy – it's easy to be generous and give away things that are in continuous supply. The more you've enjoyed being by yourself and have learned about yourself, the more willing you will be to share yourself with others.

My own advice to you would be this:

- ♥ Live every day to the fullest, as if it were your last.
- ♥ Actively demonstrate the values with which you find meaning and purpose in your life.
- ♥ Remember that pain and worry is caused not by what happens to you, but by your interpretation of what is happening to you.
- ♥ Count your blessings, and what you have got in your life, in order to direct your focus on something other than your challenges.
- ♥ Believe that you can turn any poison into medicine by looking for the lesson that your experiences are trying to teach you.
- ♥ Determine to live up to being the vibrant, sexy, compelling and admirable woman that you truly are – and never again allow anyone else to tell you differently!

Whether you remain contentedly single for the rest of your life, experience the adventure of many transitional relationships, or find your soulmate – be joyous. Good luck.

Further Reading

Andreas, Connirae Ph.D., and Andreas, Steve MA, *Heart of the Mind: Engaging Your Inner Power to Change with Neuro Linguistic Programming*, Real People Press, 1989.

Bach, David, *Smart Women Finish Rich*, Broadway Books, 1999.

Bander, Richard, and Grinder, John, *Reframing: Neuro-Linguistic Programming and the Transformation of Meaning*, Real People Press, 1982.

Barbach, Lonnie Garfield, *For Yourself: The Fulfilment of Female Sexuality*, Anchor Books, 1976.

Bay, Tony, and Macpherson, David, *Change your Attitude: Creating Success One Thought at a Time*, Career Press, 1998.

Butler, Gillian Ph.D., and Hope, Tony MD, *Managing Your Mind – The Mental Fitness Guide*, Oxford University Press, 1995.

Carter, Steven, and Sokol, Julia, *He's Scared, She's Scared*, Dell, 1993.

Carter-Scott, Cherie Ph.D., *If Love is a Game, These are the Rules*, Broadway Books, 1999.

DeAngelis, Barbara, Ph.D., *Real Moments*, Dell, 1994.

Dodson, Betty, Ph.D., *Sex for One: The Joy of Selfloving*, Three Rivers Press, 1996.

Dowrick, Stephanie, *Intimacy and Solitude*, The Women's Press, 1992.

Edwards, Gill, *Pure Bliss: The Art of Living in Soft Time*, Piatkus Books, 1999.

Engel, Beverley, *Raising Your Sexual Self-Esteem: How to Feel Better about Your Sexuality and Yourself*, Fawcett Columbine, 1995.

Graff, E. J., *What is Marriage? The Strange Social History of Our Most Intimate Institution*, Beacon Press, 1999.

Greenberger, Dennis Ph.D., and Padesky, Christine A. Ph.D., *Mind over Mood: Change How You Feel by Changing the Way You Think*, Guildford Press, 1996.

Jaycox, Victoria, *Single Again: A Guide for Women Starting Over*, W. W. Norton & Co., 1999.

Kantor, David Ph.D., *My Lover, Myself: Self-discovery through Relationship*, Riverhead Books, 1999.

Kingma, Daphne Rose, *Coming Apart: Why Relationships End and How to Live Through the Ending of Yours*, Ballantine, 1987.

Kingma, Daphne Rose, *Finding True Love*, Conari Press, 1996.

Knight, Lindsay, *Why Feeling Bad is Good*, Hodder & Stoughton, 1996.

Norwood, Robin, *Women Who Love Too Much*, Pocket Books, 1985.

Pfeiffer, Vera, *Positively Single: The Art of Being Single and Happy*, Element Books, 1991.

Rutkowski, Ken, *Happy Between Relationships*, McAlpine Press, 1999.

Schaeffer, Brenda, *Is it Love or Is it Addiction?*, Hazelden, 1987.

Simpson, Liz, *Working from the Heart*, Vermilion, 1999.

Simpson, Liz, *Finding Fulfilment*, Piatkus, 2000.

Sweet, Corinne, *Overcoming Addiction*, Piatkus, 1994.

Wilks, Frances, *Intelligent Emotion*, William Heinemann, 1998.

How to Contact the Author

Liz Simpson is a personal coach, motivational speaker and work-shop facilitator with a passion for helping individuals move from where they are to where they want to be, particularly in the areas of:

- relationships
- work/career
- finances
- self-awareness/self-esteem

If you would like to contact Liz or receive information about her personal coaching sessions and forthcoming events – both in the UK and USA – please access her website on: www.HeartWork.com or email Liz on: info@heartwork.com

Index

Other Help Yourself titles:

Come Alive
Your Six Point Plan for Lasting Health and Energy

Beth MacEoin

Do you feel below par most of the time, not ill enough to visit your GP, but lacking the energy and vitality you need to live life to the full, looking and feeling your best? *Come Alive* offers a six point plan which is radical yet achievable and which cuts through much of the current advice on health issues which can seem confusing, contradictory or downright impossible.

* How to boost your physical, mental and emotional energy
* How to strengthen your immune system in mind and body
* How to adopt an eating plan that is delicious and healthy
* How to exercise enough for great fitness with minimum effort
* How to value relaxation and positive thinking
* How to limit the damage when life goes off the rails

Published by Contemporary Books
ISBN 0-658-01476-5

Get Everything Done

And Still Have Time to Play

Mark Forster

Time is what our lives are made of and yet our failure to use time properly can have disastrous effects on our happiness and sense of well-being. This book is written for everyone who has to juggle different demands in a busy schedule, including advice on finding an effective system while making allowances for human psychology and the unexpected. Forster points out that the key to success lies in repeated, consistent and focused action and shows us how to put this into practice in order to maximise our enjoyment of work and leisure.

- Getting moving – how to overcome resistance and procrastination
- Time allocation – scheduling work-time and free-time
- Making the maximum possible use of the time available
- Coping with interruptions and emergencies
- The number one time management tool: Saying 'No'

Published by Contemporary Books
ISBN 0-658-02150-8

Get the Happiness Habit

How You Can Choose Your Steps to a Happy Life

Christine Webber

Happiness is a natural force within us. But sometimes we
have to relearn it. It seems that at some point in our lives we
lose the gift of being happy and are constantly struggling
to find that elusive joy. This inspiring book discourages the
illusion that happiness can be bought or acquired or will
magically happen. Instead it shows that happiness is an inner
choice and that with a bit of skill and a mind shift,
life will never be the same again.

- Assess your own happiness
- Learn the secrets of happy people
- Rethink those irrational, negative beliefs
- Stop feeling guilty
- Know that you deserve to be happy
- Act happy – be happy

Published by Contemporary Books
ISBN 0-658-01478-1